U.S. Customs

U.S. Customs

Badge of Dishonor

Darlene Fitzgerald-Catalan

Authors Choice Press
San Jose New York Lincoln Shanghai

U.S. Customs
Badge of Dishonor

Authors Choice Press
an imprint of iUniverse, Inc.

For information address:
iUniverse, Inc.
5220 S. 16th St., Suite 200
Lincoln, NE 68512
www.iuniverse.com

Author photo courtesy of Ernie Bach and KISS Photo.

ISBN: 0-595-16795-0

Printed in the United States of America

Dedication

I dedicate this book to all of the women and men in the Department of The Treasury who have, and are currently fighting the corrupt "Good Old Boy", crony system, and have suffered as they chose to make a stand against it.

To my dad Kelsie, a World War II Veteran and survivor of the battle of Guadal Cannel, who taught me that the only thing worse than fear, is regret.

To Ian Lawler and Ben Catalan. Thank you so much Ben for your undying support, and your superb intellect. You are my bridge over troubled water.

Contents

One Clear Voice

Foreword—by Gary Aldrich

For more than 26 years I served as a special agent with the federal bureau of investigation. Part of my responsibility was to study, then attack the Mafia and other organized crime groups. All organized crime, or "OC," had similarities that enabled criminals to avoid detection and capture. One useful tool was "Omerta"—the Mafia-inspired code of silence—that ordered secrecy so that "outsiders" could not learn of their criminal conspiracies and illegal activities, and weaknesses.

The classic way to maintain Omerta is to warn each member of the group that terrible things will happen to them if they violate the groups' secrecy rules. For example, it is routine inside the Mafia and other violent OC groups to torture, then kill suspected "rats" who disclose information to the wrong persons—such as law enforcement officers. Even if the "rat" or "stool pigeon" makes the disclosure accidentally, or with the best of intentions, the punishment is the same—torture, then death.

Sometimes the OC members are so angry, they destroy the "whistle blower's" entire family. Or to make a point with a suspected "leaker," they may threaten, kill, or kidnap one of the "boat-rocker's" children. This is how they enforce the silence that protects them all.

After the "informant" is very publicly punished, anybody else who might have been thinking of disclosing information to outsiders will think twice, thus, the blanket of protective secrecy is maintained.

When I went to work for the FBI there was another kind of silence in place. It was called the "Secrets Act" or some such official sounding name. There was also a group ethic in play that is fairly common in law enforcement. I was told in the strongest terms that nothing I learned on the job could be disclosed, except to prosecutors, judges and juries. Only the facts that I gathered to convict criminals could be disclosed, and if we had any corruption or incompetence inside the agency, we were to handle our "dirty laundry" ourselves, and not let anyone else know about it.

That was the group ethic then, and I suspect it is the same way now. These twisted ethics fostered a "them against us" mentality. Such foxhole mentality helps to bond workers together but can be dangerous if serious corruption is discovered. If there is a pattern of cover-up, who decides what gets to be hidden and what needs to be revealed? In the last years of my career, I witnessed significant damage to national security and to the reputation of the FBI as my agency bent over backwards for political reasons to please a reckless president and his corrupted administration.

Historically, the FBI has even forbidden the disclosure of information to immediate family members. Moreover, FBI agents could not disclose serious wrongdoing to their own attorneys, unless they first sought and received permission from the FBI. If they violated this rule, they were subject to dismissal for insubordination.

Federal agents were never to speak to the media, unless they had permission, and then such occasions were closely monitored by management. Even when FBI special agents were called to testify in front of congressional oversight committees they were not able to speak candidly—they were accompanied by agency attorneys, ever ready to lower the boom if the agent's remarks were not part of the "party line" desired by the "front office." Agents deemed to be overly talkative were considered "disloyal" to the agency and director, and upper management was promptly notified about such lapses. When agents spoke to "outsiders" it was a well-known fact that careers hung in the balance.

It was the "kiss of death" to an FBI agent's career if it was learned that they had independently complained to their own Senator or Representative about FBI missteps or shortcomings. Even if perfectly legal and highly useful to the Legislative Branch's oversight responsibilities, such contacts were and still are deemed to be disloyal and highly suspicious to the rest of the FBI group—especially the management.

Some of this secrecy may be good, because secrecy protects national security and also protects important cases under investigation. After all, nobody wants the "bad guys" to learn about progress of the investigation, or weaknesses in any particular case. This is especially true today when our nation is under attack by foreign terrorists. Everyone understands that a certain amount of information should remain confidential.

It is also a truism that management is better informed and thus logically should be the group to officially disclose agency matters. But, what if management is a big part of the problem? Can we not assume that they would be less candid when called to answer?

There is a difference between protecting secrets that bear on investigations or national security, and hiding information that may indicate a deep incompetence or corruption.

Furthermore, human beings are naturally eager to hide their shortcomings because they know if their flaws are available for review by higher management their careers will not be enhanced. They know they are better off, career-wise if they are able to cover-up missteps and stupidity.

Agency chiefs also know that they will be scolded and held responsible if agents under their control make mistakes or become corrupted. So, "keeping the lid on" is part of the "group-think" that eventually takes over any bureaucracy—no matter how honest and decent the group was when it was first organized.

Most citizens do not realize this. Most honest, decent applicants who decide to make federal law enforcement their lifelong career are totally unaware of this. It's ironic that federal law enforcement agencies spend millions of dollars each year to find honest applicants. They consider honesty and integrity as major requirements for successful completion of the applicant process, but once hired they indoctrinate new recruits into the ethic of the group, which includes the code of silence—the "ethic" of Omerta, the concept of a cover-up.

In some cases, newly minted honest federal law enforcement officers do not even complete academy training before they are faced with their first dilemma: to report untoward, unethical activity. Whether it's the cover-up of a simple-minded instructor who "hits" on the attractive new female recruits, or it's the inappropriate activities of fellow officers during their off-duty time, or even something more serious—the conflict between becoming a whistle blower, or "going along to get along" begins early in each federal agent's career, and continues on until the day they resign, or retire.

Most always, such corruptions or lapses are minor in nature and can be overlooked without serious impact to the quality of the group, or to the mission of the agency.

But, increasingly—and for reasons that go far beyond my ability to explain in a mere book foreword—serious corruptions and instances of incompetence, "good-old-boy isms," blatant examples of "careerism," and other destructive group-think activities have become a serious factor in the careers of too many good, hardworking, decent and yes—honest—federal law enforcement officers' daily routines.

And all too often, federal agents spend as much time watching their backs for attacks from stupid or jealous management as they do working on the mission of putting the bad guys out of business.

It has become the reflexive response of every single federal agency, especially federal law enforcement, to attack the messenger—to attack the whistle blower who dares to come forward to question the low quality of management or work performance. Even when they try to surface serious corruption, or protect national security weakened on purpose, or by accident, whistle blowers are treated as pariahs, not worthy of sitting at the same lunch table with decent people.

The FBI has made some small progress since I came forward in 1996. This is exhibited in the respectful treatment of honest ethical dissenters, and with the taking of their complaints more seriously. A new FBI director was just appointed and it is hoped that he will be able to address the FBI's many management shortcomings. We will watch, and we will hope. Still, I've never seen a whistle blower publicly saluted by any FBI director, or any other director of any other federal law enforcement agency.

How did it get this way? How can we fix it? Why don't we celebrate those who are trying to make things better? Why do we allow bureaucrats free reign to punish these beleaguered, honest and courageous public servants who come forward?

I don't have all the answers. All I know is that U.S. Customs agent Darlene Fitzgerald-Catalan and her loyal associates in the federal law enforcement agency in which they served, ran up against tremendous incompetence, and quite possibly a major corruption in the management ranks of those who are supposed to protect our borders.

They tried to work within the system, as they were trained and told to do. Then they went to their legal representatives, who amazingly betrayed them. Then they went public, just as I had done before. I survived being a whistle blower, and then I prospered—and so will Darlene and her brave friends, with our help.

It is every citizen's responsibility to support our "ethical dissenters," those honest citizens who step forward to shine a light on that which is so obviously wrong. Some day the federal government will be forced to abandon the ethics of the Mafia—as it pertains to the disclosures of honest federal employees who are simply trying to right a serious wrong.

Sadly, I believe that will only happen after the general population loses its twisted fascination and affections for corrupt (if "cute") politicians, other kinds of pirates, anti-heroes, and the Mafia.

But until that happens, our ethical dissenters will find their strongest support among the decent law abiding members of our society who know the difference between the protection of national security—and the maintenance of a system of silence. Such enforced silence is nothing more than shelter for the incompetent and the corrupted, who gleefully feed at the public trough.

Thank you, former US Customs agent Darlene Fitzgerald-Catalan. Your country owes you a debt of gratitude for stepping forward. You protected your country in the military. You wore a gun and badge and protected us along the borders. Your revelations continue to protect us all.

Foreword

When Darlene Catalan and I first met in 1989, we were both Special Agents with the U.S. Customs Service in Los Angeles, California. Back then, in our late 20's, we were idealistic federal agents eager to do our jobs and who believed wholeheartedly in the U.S. Customs Service Mission…to investigate and prosecute violators of Customs laws. To us and all other agents we worked with, the bad guys were the outsiders and so forth. And in the early years of our careers, that was indeed the case. Though we worked in different offices and saw each other on occasional surveillances or training days, we both achieved a great deal of recognition for our strong abilities as investigators and learned what it took to go after the big boys in the world of drug smuggling and money laundering. Over the years, we became the closest of friends.

Beginning in December 1997, our world and our belief in the Agency we had devoted our lives began to disintegrate right in front of our eyes. How could Darlene and I have known or even imagined the events which would descend upon us when we chose to exercise our rights under the law and engage in an administrative process under the Equal Employment Opportunity Commission (EEOC)? How could we have known that from that moment forward and even up to this date in January 2001, our lives would be intertwined in a series of events which would result in us battling corruption and criminal activity at the highest levels within the U.S. Customs Service alongside several other courageous Customs employees who chose to exercise their integrity in defiance of the lies and deceit of Customs managers and their cronies? From that moment forward, none of our lives would ever be the same. We would be harassed, threatened, intimidated, investigated by Internal Affairs on false charges, surveilled electronically, surveilled by agents within our own agency, and ultimately forced to choose our own resignations from a job we had once dearly loved just to keep our honor and integrity intact.

There are those who say we gave up the fight by resigning in September 1999. And for the corrupt management officials we found ourselves battling against, they applauded their victory thinking that was the last they would ever hear of Darlene Catalan and Sandy Nunn. Neither of these groups was correct. For Darlene and I are not and never will be quitters. It's not in our blood. It was ingrained in us from the day we were born as daughters of highly decorated military officers. Darlene's father was a World War II veteran and a survivor of the Battle of Guaddel Canal. Mine was an Air force pilot. No, we didn't resign just to quit and give up the fight. We resigned to keep our integrity and as a protest to the abusive treatment we were being subjected to on a daily basis at the hands of corrupt managers who were abusing their authority and openly violating federal laws in the process.

It has been over a year and a half since we resigned from our positions with Customs. But, giving up was never an option for us. We have committed ourselves to bringing the truth out to the people of this country because it is the right thing to do and our sense of integrity compels us to do so. Darlene has taken the first step in doing so by writing this book and describing in personal detail the abuse we were subjected to and the jeopardy our lives were placed in when we uncovered corruption of unimaginable proportions in one of the most powerful federal law enforcement agencies in the U.S.—the U.S. Customs Service. Darlene's account of the events and the people involved is both accurate and bone chilling to those of us who experienced these events first-hand. I highly encourage each and every taxpayer and American to read this book and know that, though some of the names have been changed, the facts themselves are absolutely true. When you are finished reading this account of what really goes on within the U.S. Customs Service, ask yourselves this: "If they can do this to federal agents within their own agency and get away with it, what could they do to me?" Think about that. Customs has the broadest search authority of any agency in the United States and their abusive practices towards their employees are beginning to spill into the public sector as evidenced by recent legal problems they've been experiencing because of illegal searches of people re-entering the U.S. from foreign destinations.

The fact remains that the U.S. Customs service is clearly a federal agency that abuses its authority both to its employees and to the public at large. It is an agency that has gone through enormous trouble to hide its problems to Congress and to you, the taxpayer. It is an agency rife with corrupt management officials and their cronies. Clearly, it is an agency in serious need of an intensive GAO investigation, serious internal reform, in serious need of removal of hundreds of corrupt managers (either through jail terms or termination), and strict oversight by Congress and the taxpayers of this country. This agency has become arrogant in its practices and the time has come for it to stop. The taxpayers of this country and the remaining good, decent, honest employees within the agency deserve much more than what they are currently getting.

Read this book! Take the time to read the book by Cathy Harris, "Flying While Black: A Whistleblower's Story" of how Cathy, a Customs Inspector from Atlanta, Georgia blew the whistle on illegal search practices by Customs officials towards returning minorities from foreign destinations. And in the coming months, read my account of the national issue in my upcoming book, "The Dark Side of Justice." All in all, you will begin to learn just how great this issue really is and how it affects your family and your business.

It is said that "Knowledge is power." This is truly the case. We were the true insiders who saw the reality of corruption first-hand. We are trying to change that by educating those of you who will read these accounts, listen and take a hand in bringing integrity back to federal law enforcement before the corruption becomes so great it deteriorates our system of government and federal law enforcement agencies forever.

SANDY G. NUNN
President/CEO, Mirsan Consulting Group
National Spokeswoman, Association of Customs Employees for Change
Former Special Agent, U.S. Customs Service 1989-1999

Acknowledgements

I would like to give special thanks to my family who stood by me through the enormous stress this battle created upon them. I also want to thank my parents who taught me to face life with a spine, and I apologize for all the worry I caused them.

I would like to thank the brave woman and men who stood shoulder to shoulder with me, and fought bravely against corruption, cronyism, discrimination, and the glass ceiling within the U.S. Customs Service. These individuals endured tremendous stress that can best be described as similar to that created by a war. To Ruben Sandoval, Sandy Nunn, Ervin Rios, Cynthia Gonyea, Renado Gianini, Ricardo Sandoval, John Carmon, and Cathy Harris, I am proud of each one of you for growing a spine, and taking your best shot at the "MAFIA" style of management indelibly in place within the United States Customs Service. I know that this courage cost all of us dearly.

To our attorneys, Gastone Beebe and Thomas Allison, thank you for believing in all of us, and for putting up with our many phone calls and insistent behavior. Thank you for educating all of us to our rights as federal employees, and to how the EEO "SYSTEM" is really designed to work only on behalf of the "MAFIA" style of management employed in the U.S. Customs Service.

Special thanks to Gary Aldrich (author of UNLIMITED ACCESS) and his staff at the Patrick Henry Foundation. I commend you and your foundation for the courage and support that you provide to honest cops attempting to get positive change in their agencies. You are brave soldiers and a credit to the spirit that your foundation represents "Give Me Liberty or Give Me Death!"

To the brave attorneys of the Government Accountability Project (GAP), a special note of appreciation. Your efforts in assisting whistle-blowers through proposing much needed legislation is a demonstration of honor.

Special thanks to Sandy Nunn, Gary Aldrich, and Sarah Barbour for assisting with the final editing of this book. Their literary skills made this book much more legible to the average "non-law enforcement" person. And to Ernie Bach of KISS Photo for his assistance in the creation of the graphics for this book.

Introduction

This book is based on a true story, as seen through the eyes of a female federal agent Darlene Catalan. Darlene tells of how federal agents in the Department of Treasury, U.S. Customs Service, fought a courageous battle against cronyism, fraud, discrimination, and corruption. Most of the names in this story have been changed, names of cases/operations have been changed, some characters have been combined, and the sequences of events have been altered. This was done in order to protect innocent agents who are still working for Customs, the pending federal civil litigation against the Customs Service, as well as confidential informants/sources and ongoing related criminal cases.

Chapter 1

The Murder

December 17, 1990, Attorney/Private Investigator Jason Fielding with his daughter Megan, was driving home from Megan's school play, in Long Beach, California. Jason was an attorney, and a well respected private investigator. Jason had been working on an investigation for a special Congressional committee in Washington, D.C. for the past 180 days. He had come home for a much-needed Christmas Break, and to see his daughter in her first school play.

Jason was 44-years-old, and a well respected, seasoned investigator who had been hand-picked for special assignments for the government. This investigation involved allegations of corruption in the U.S. Customs Service. Jason and his wife, Anita, had been married for 7 years, and had a beautiful home in Long Beach. Anita, a computer programmer, missed her husband terribly when he was gone. However, she was particularly tolerant of this last assignment because she knew that soon her husband would be home for good.

Anita had decided to stay behind at the auditorium to help the teachers clean up after the play. The plan was for Jason to drive six year old Megan home, feed her, spend time with her, and tuck her in bed. Then he and Anita could have some quality time alone together. Jason was a good man who loved his family very much. Megan was the apple of his eye. There has never been a child more loved by its father than Megan, and Megan adored her daddy.

The drive home from Megan's play was full of fun and magic. Jason was an amateur magician and would always perform his tricks for his daughter, who idolized him. After a quick trip through the drive-up window at Burger King, off for home they went. Jason opened his mouth wide while Megan tried to throw French fries in her dad's mouth. She hit him in the eye, and they both cracked up. It was a cool, crisp Long Beach December, and Jason could taste the seawater on his lips as they drew closer to the ocean. It felt good to be home.

As Jason pulled the car in their driveway, the security (night-censored) lights went on. Jason helped Megan with her seatbelt, and the two of them grabbed up the bags of fast food, and exited the vehicle. Jason had his hands full, and pushed the car door shut with his foot. He never saw the darkly dressed, masked man come from behind the bushes. Megan gasped quickly drawing her father's attention towards her. Jason thought that Megan had closed her hand in the car door. Just then, three muffled shots quickly filled the air. As Megan watched in shock, her daddy collapsed to the ground like a bag of sand, and the life drifted from him. Jason looked up at her in sorrow as if his last thoughts were of how tragic that his baby daughter had to see this traumatic thing. As Megan cried, the perpetrator fled.

Chapter 2

EEO

On November 11, 1996, Renado Gianini and I were on surveillance on Mill Street in San Bernardino, California. I was running an operation called Operation Black Widow with the San Bernardino Police Department, and the Special Agents (SA's) of the Union Pacific (UP), and Burlington Northern/Santa Fe (BNSF) Railroads. We had a confidential informant (CI) that had given us information that this organization of thugs was hitting railroad boxcars as they were entering into Redlands and San Bernardino. So far that year, they had made off with approximately 11 million dollars of Custom's in-bond merchandise. This same ring was supposed to be involved in the manufacturing/distribution of Methamphetamine (meth/speed). We also learned that right in the middle of all of this was a crooked border patrol officer. We had been surveilling this particular crook who had been seen meeting with the border patrol officer for several days now, putting together enough P.C. (probable cause) to hit two suspected stash houses.

I was parked in an abandoned warehouse on Norton Air Force Base, looking through binoculars at the crooks house on Mill Street. Renado was sitting a couple of blocks over, with several other officers from his department. As I sat there it hit me that my very first case with Customs was just down the street. That's how I met Renado Gianini. We ended up seizing 72 million dollars of precursors and lab equipment for manufacturing meth on that caper. I remembered how different Renado looked then, all narced out. His hair was long, he sported an earring, and he basically looked like a thug. This was his U.C. (Undercover look). Renado was a very muscular, white male, with red hair, mustache, about 45-yrs-old, and handsome in a very rugged way. Now he wears a suit and tie most of the time, and I can hardly get him in the field with me. As I thought of this, I began to laugh. Then I recalled how that case was one of the first of many very large seizures that I would make, with no recognition from management of my work. I remembered how hurt I was to find out that, unlike others in my office, I would receive no type of award or recognition at all regarding this case, and how that's when a lot of this crap got started for me. My laughter turned to a headache.

Just then a van departed the residence and we continued surveilling as it moved to a couple of locations dropping off stolen merchandise. A couple of hours later, Renado had the state warrant in hand and we began kicking doors. The first door we went into was the main residence of our primary subject. As Renado took him to the floor and handcuffed him, another guy ran out the back door. Another TFO (Task Force Officer) named Ray and I chased after him. We ran and ran. I saw that the subject was overweight and wasn't going to last long. I began just pacing him. I was in good running shape, and didn't want to catch up with him too quickly; I thought it better to let him wear himself down first. After a few minutes, he was so out of breath he fell to the ground, and I pounced on him. I secured the cuffs, and sat on him to catch my breath. I started laughing and said, "Well fat boy, you better go on a diet if you're gonna stay in this line of work, you made this too easy for me." About that time TFO Ray, also out of shape, caught up. The search at that location yielded about $500,000 dollars of stolen merchandise (T.V.'s, designer clothes, V.C.R.'s, exercise equipment) taken from the railroad.

We proceeded to the second location. We entered this "Ghetto Dive" apartment complex, and walked on foot through this tiny walkway between two walls. At the end, there was a cast-iron gate. As we approached, a large black kid, about 15 years old wearing an old army field jacket opened the gate and walked towards us. The TFO that I was with said to him, "hay partner, would you hold the gate open for us please." The kid saw our raid gear and badges, gave us a dirty look and slammed the gate behind him, inhibiting our entrance. I had seen this look a hundred times before; that "I hate you" look of pure resentment and wrongful displacement of rage for a life with little hope. Just as he slammed the gate shut, the TFO and I both noticed what appeared to be the end of a rifle sticking out of his jacket sleeve. The TFO yelled, "Gun!" and we both grabbed him and pushed him to the wall.

Renado ran up to us, and grabbed the guy too. The TFO and Renado pinned each of his shoulders against the wall, while I grabbed at the object in his jacket, and pulled out a riflescope. My immediate thought was that where there's a scope, there's a gun. Just then, the subject tried to jerk away and attempted to reach under his jacket. We were in a little alleyway, with no more than 4 ft between each wall; it was a tight situation. As Renado and the TFO tried to push his shoulders back against the wall and control his arms, I tried to beat him to the gun. Grabbing his jacket, I pulled the bottom of it up and felt inside his belt area. Sure enough, there was a pistol sticking halfway out of the front of his pants. I looked at Renado and said "gun". Renado grabbed the guy's arm and tried to wrench it behind him in an effort to stand him up straight so that I could grab the gun. I grabbed the gun, and the guy lunged fore-word and bent over, trapping my hand on the gun in his belt. The suspect really started fighting us, trying to reach for the gun. He was looking at me with such intensity. I sensed that he was determined to get the gun and blow my head off. My hand was caught in his belt, and I could feel my bones being crushed.

I knew that I had to get this gun before he broke my hand and got it. I pressed my feet against the adjacent wall, and pushed my shoulder into his chest in an effort to straighten out his torso. As I was pushing against him with all my might, I could feel my heart racing, and my chest pounding. As I pressed my shoulder and head into him, I felt the energy draining from my body and my hand crushing. I think that my mind started wondering as a defense mechanism for blocking out the pain. I started seeing flashes of green grass waving in the wind, and I could hear my kids laughing. Just then Renado screamed, "Get the gun Dar! Get the gun!" A sudden rush of adrenaline pounded through my body, and I gave one last powerful push against the wall, pulling the gun out. The gun went flying, and I jumped, securing it. We then wrestled the guy to his knees and cuffed him. As we caught our breath, I looked at Renado. He was starring at me like the cat that caught the cannery. "What?" I asked. Renado said jokingly "You just had to get your hands down a man's pants today somehow, didn't you." I got up, and pushed Renado off balance, so that he fell over laughing. Renado knew that only he and Ruben (my Customs partner) could ever get away with that kind of joking around with me. They were like brothers to me.

As we finished processing the evidence and booking the crooks, Renado said, "So, you and Ruben are really going to do this tomorrow, huh?" I looked at him uncertainly and said, "Looks like it." Renado said, "Well Dar, for what it's worth, I think you guys are doing the right thing. It takes a lot of guts to do what you guys are doing. I know that in most agencies those complaints aren't received that well, to say the least." He shook my hand, and I smiled. That night I could hardly sleep. I was still pumped up over having to fight a 15-year-old gang-banger for a gun, and even more worried about what Ruben and I were about to do tomorrow.

On November 12, 1996, my partner Special Agent Ruben Sandoval and I went to the World Trade Center in Long Beach to meet with the EEO (Equal Employment Opportunity) Counselor on Ruben's EEO complaint. I was Ruben's key witness to the discrimination dealt him for several years, at the hands of our group supervisor Ivan Winkowsky. As bad as I thought Winkowsky had treated me for not being a man, I knew that it wasn't half as bad as his obvious discrimination against

Ruben for being Latino. Ruben and I had been partners/office-mates for about 6 years. Prior to Customs, Ruben spent 7 years with Secret Service, and 7 years with Fontana Police Department as a dog handler. Rubin was 41 years old, about 5ft 10in tall, and a well built, handsome Latin male. Ruben was an excellent agent, with a street savvy confidence, and ESP about him that kept us out of trouble on more than one occasion. I remember how nervous and out of character Ruben was about meeting with this EEO counselor. It was as if his street wise ESP was kicking in, and we were both choosing to ignore it for the first time, a mistake we'd later regret.

The EEO counselor was a young black agent named Victor Ross. Ruben and I told him of all the unfairness that had been going on at the RAIC (Resident Agent In Charge) Riverside office for several years. I was surprised that he highly recommended we retain an attorney. I didn't think much about this at the time, but if I knew then what I know now, I would have listened closer to his advice and retained an attorney much sooner. Now I know that these words were not just simple advice, but a subtle warning.

Mr. Ross also recommended that we consider filing a class action EEO complaint and that we talk to the EEO supervisor Ms. Mary Conales. Her office was just down the hall, so after our interview we stopped by her office to talk. Ms. Conales was a very beautiful, long-haired, Latin woman, in her late twenties. My very first impression of her was that she was sneaky and coy. Her mannerisms, and jesters reminded me of a Latin version of Scarlet O'Hara, in "Gone With the Wind," a little slippery vixen. We told Ms. Conales that we were interested in filing a Class EEO complaint. We explained to her what had been going on at the RAIC (Resident Agent In Charge) /Riverside, the small field office where we worked, and that Ruben had already filed an individual EEO complaint. I told her that I too had intended on filing a complaint, but would consider filing a class action if it was more appropriate. She played ignorant, and acted like she didn't know much about the class complaint system. I saw red flags and immediately started to distrust her. I thought to myself, she is a supervisor, why the hell doesn't she know anything about class EEO complaints? She told us that she would research it and get back to us. When we left her office, I knew that her ignorance of EEO policies was just an act, and I began to worry.

Chapter 3

The Threats Begin

On November 30, 1996, SAIC (Special Agent In Charge, Los Angeles, CA) Drake Brinkley spoke at a congratulatory pizza party for all those persons recently promoted. *Drake Brinkley* was the agent in charge of the large *Office of Investigations for all of Los Angeles*, as well as several RAIC's (smaller satellite field offices), in southern California, Las Vegas and Nevada. Drake Brinkley was a white male, approximately 49-years-old and appeared rather unassuming, and of no consequence. The congratulatory speech that Brinkley was giving regarded the recent promotion in which Ruben and I had been passed over; while agents with much less experience, less time with Customs, and much less significant casework, were promoted. These agents also happened to be white males, no coincidence or shocking news for the Customs Agency. Brinkley arrogantly announced to all attendees, "Someone at the RAIC/Riverside has filed a grievance, and now I have to deal with them." I had the wisdom not to attend this party, but was told of Brinkley's subtle threat. I wondered how Brinkley knew so quickly that we had filed a complaint. Ruben's complaint was still at the informal/anonymous stage, and was by EEO policies, supposed to be confidential. My suspicions immediately turned to Mary Conales. I knew I had pegged her right.

On December 4, 1996, our Group Supervisor, Ivan Winkowsky, posted an e-mail message from Donald Chin on the bulletin board in the entry way of our office for everyone to see. Ivan Winkowsky was one of our office group supervisors. Winkowsky was about 48-yrs-old, white male, big nose, and looked and acted rather dopey. Not the type of guy that would have any kind of presence or regal demeanor as he walked into a room. The message Winkowsky posted stated, "For anyone who is experiencing any problems at the RAIC/Riverside, the preferred method of reporting problems is by using the chain-of-command." On the memo hanging on the bulletin board at the RAIC/Riverside, someone had written the word "one" on the memo, to indicate that there was only one person having a problem at the RAIC/Riverside. I immediately recognized the handwriting as being the office brown-noser, and weasel, Edwin Easel.

A cross between the T.V. character Frank Burns from MASH and ex-Vice President Dan Quayl, Easel the Weasel, as we commonly referred to him, couldn't investigate his way out of a paper bag. This mattered not to Customs management, because he was still white male, and one of the "good old boys". Weasel was average height and weight, but very handsome in an impish sort of way. He spent an inordinate amount of time in Winkowsky's office, getting cases spoon-fed to him. He had no prior law enforcement background, unlike Ruben and I, and hadn't made any significant cases on his own. Winkowsky ate this guy up buying his ""kiss ass" act, hook, line, and sinker. Winkowsky was cut from the same cloth. He moved up in the "Customs Crony System" much in the same way that most white male agents did. It was never about what you did, but who you knew, and if you were the right gender and color. That was common knowledge throughout the agency, and Ruben and I naively thought that we could actually change things.

I was furious when I saw this e-mail message posted. Any anonymity that Ruben should have retained, went right out the window. When I showed it to Ruben, I could see the anger and concern on his face. Ruben is the last of the hard-core cops. He always reveals only the tough cop demeanor on the job, but I have seen this tough guy with his kids, coaching little league, and the softy in him couldn't help from coming out. I have also seen the lighter side of Ruben in his concern for my well-being. Ruben and my husband had become fast friends, and they loved to enjoy themselves (jokingly) at my expense. When Ruben and I partnered up and became office cellmates, I could tell he was leery of working with a woman at first. It took me a while to earn his respect and trust, but it was worth it.

The next day, I noticed that Winkowsky had left for lunch, and had foolishly left his checkbook on his desk. I took the next check out of his book, grabbed a quick lunch and waited for his return. I let Bob (Robert Mattivi) in on the joke that I was about to play on Winkowsky. Winkowsky had previously enlightened the office that he was often angry about how his wife spends money. He always complained about her to us, and I would think, what a controlling asshole he was. This poor woman always had to either sneak checks from him or to ask this jerk permission to spend money. How Winkowsky treated his wife was a big indicator to me of just how Winkowsky viewed women and their place in life. Winkowsky was the quintessential male chauvinist pig, and he disgusted me. When Winkowsky returned from lunch, I was in the back office where he couldn't see me. I disguised my voice, and placed a call to Winkowsky. I explained to Winkowsky that I was from his bank, and was just checking for clearance to use his overdraft protection for the check we had just received for $7,000 dollars. He fell for my act, and I could hear Winkowsky grab his checkbook and thumb through it in a panic. I gave him the check number, and told him that it was signed by a Pamela Winkowsky (his wife). I told him that normally we didn't call for overdraft protection, but because it was for such a large amount and he'd never used his overdraft before, I thought it looked suspicious.

I could just feel Winkowsky having a stroke over the phone. He said, in a frantic tone of voice, "No, No, I'm not authorizing this." I responded with, "Well Mr. Winkowsky, I'm not here to ascertain if you gave her permission sir, only to verify if this is your wife's signature." He said, "Well yeah, but I never authorized this amount." I told him, "Well sir, she is on your joint account, and I was just verifying that she did in fact sign this check, she doesn't need your authorization." You could hear Winkowsky breathing hard as he stuttered, "Just, just hold on a minute, just hold on," and he put me on hold. I then walked up the hall, just short of his office as he was drastically dialing the phone, cussing his wife with a stream of obscenities as he dialed. Bob and I started busting up laughing. Just then, Winkowsky looked at us laughing in his doorway, and caught on to the joke as I waived his check back and forth. Bob took one look at Winkowsky's face, and started howling, "Oh Darlene, ha, ha, ha, this was the funniest thing I'd ever seen. Oh Dar, that was great, I'm going to have a stroke! Ha ha, ha." Winkowsky was so pissed off, he started cussing us both out. Bob and I laughed so hard I thought we both would just die. We fell down on Winkowsky's couch dying laughing. Then Winkowsky, realizing that his wife didn't spend $7,000 dollars, started laughing with us just a little. This would be the last time that I would ever laugh with Winkowsky about anything.

Later that day, I began calling Ms. Conales in attempt to get information about the class EEO complaint. Although I left numerous messages, she never called me back. I finally felt sure that she was stringing me along, so I called her secretary and made an appointment. I knew that I had pegged this witch right.

On December 7, 1996, I took a day off work, and drove a three (3) hour commute into Long Beach for my meeting with Ms. Conales. She still claimed not to have the necessary information on how to instruct me to file a class EEO complaint. I showed her the E-mail message posted by Winkowsky. I immediately saw her begin to squirm. I asked her how it was that SAC/LA management found out so quickly about Ruben's complaint being filed. She was extremely uncomfortable about the question and told me that she thought management must have seen Victor Ross' travel request for the trip from San Diego to Los Angeles. This answer made me even more suspicious about her. You see, the travel request for Ross wouldn't have gone through SAIC/LA's management, it would have been processed through SAC/San Diego, the office that Victor worked out of. SAC/LA wouldn't even have a reason to review it. Once again, Ms. Conales failed to properly advise me of how to file a class EEO complaint. In fact, she really was no help at all. She again assured me that she would research it and get back to me. I sensed early on that Ms. Conales was a snake. Several weeks went by and I kept calling Ms. Conales, and documenting each time I called her. She never got back to me.

Darlene with Customs Mobile X-ray van

Chapter 4

The "Good Old Boy System" hard at work

On December 17, 1996, SA Edwin Easel, and recently promoted SSA Peter Blake (tall, white male, blond hair)—after completion of a surveillance in La Verne, California—conspired not to return Narcotics evidence to the RAIC/Riverside evidence locker, against Treasury Policy. Ruben and I were supporting the case agent SA Janet Somers (short, hefty, white woman) on this case. I was inside the Mail Depot, acting as the U.C. (undercover), attempting to complete the controlled delivery of package of heroin. While scanning radio frequencies that night Ruben intercepted a conversation between Blake and Easel, which indicated to Ruben that neither of them, both being evidence custodians for our office, wanted to travel to RAIC/RV (Resident Agent In Charge, Riverside office) to secure the narcotics evidence for the night. This is a huge violation of policy, and could sacrifice the whole case based on violation of chain of custody rules and laws.

On January 9, 1997, SA Janet Somers, officially notified Group Supervisor Ivan Winkowsky, that she was of the belief that the heroin involved in her controlled delivery had been taken home on December 17 by one of the evidence custodians, and not properly placed in the evidence locker until the following A.M. Janet was obviously concerned about the upcoming trial on this case, and the effect the break in the chain of custody would have on the case. It could potentially be thrown out. Winkowsky, upon learning of this allegation, made no attempt to report this violation of Customs Policy to the Office of Internal Affairs (IA), and instead chose to cover up this incident, violating customs policy, and federal law. Winkowsky never would have covered the asses of anyone else in that office, only his crony's. Now these "Good old Boys" would owe him a favor. That's how it works in the Customs Service.

On January 29, 1997, SA Janet Somers was requested to provide her entire case file, to include file notes, to Assistant United States Attorney (AUSA) Bailey Miller. Janet was to fax this report to Miller. Janet went in to Winkowsky's office in order to again discuss her reservations about the notes present in the original case file. These notes indicated the misconduct by the evidence custodians Easel and Blake (RE: heroin going home in 1997). Janet told Winkowsky that she believed more than likely, she would be questioned over this matter by the AUSA. Janet later told Ruben that at first, Winkowsky denied that he had any knowledge of ever previously discussing this misconduct with her. Then Janet showed Winkowsky the date on her "9-B, Case Chronology and Review Form," dated January 9, 1997, where she documented the fact that she had personally made him aware of this alleged misconduct, and where Winkowsky had signed off of this 9-B on her quarterly review. Janet had Winkowsky dead to rights. Janet said that Winkowsky's memory magically returned. Following this conversation with Janet, Winkowsky, once again, failed to report this misconduct to I.A, via Treasury Policy.

On February 2, 1997, my G-ride (slang for government issued vehicle) needed to go into the shop. Ruben was on leave for a couple of days, so I grabbed the extra keys to his G-ride from the key box. I jumped into the car, and attempted to drive it. The steering was virtually out. I had been training for the 1999 Police Olympics, had extremely good upper body strength, and it was all that I could do just to cut the wheel. When I went to put on the brakes, they too were faulty. Ruben had been complaining about this car to Winkowsky for a while, and Winkowsky refused to issue him another vehicle. I couldn't believe that Ruben had been driving this piece of crap.

I parked the car and went back into the office for a different set of keys. The key box was in Winkowsky's office, behind his door. As I entered his office, Winkowsky was sitting at his desk. I gave him a condescending look and shook my head as I reached for the key box. Winkowsky said, "What are you doing?" I replied, "I'm getting another car. That piece of shit you got Ruben driving is dangerous, and you're dam lucky he hasn't gotten hurt in it." Winkowsky, in a sarcastic demeaning tone of voice said, "There's nothing wrong with that car," and made a condescending shooing motion at me. I felt my blood boiling and my face getting hot with rage. I walked over to him, leaned over his desk, and placed my face uncomfortably close to his and glared into his eyes. I slammed the keys to Ruben's car down on the desk in front of him, almost hitting his hand. He reacted startled, and jerked his back in an effort to create distance from me. My voice was low and cracking with anger as I said, "Be careful Ivan, be careful" and walked out.

I was headed out, with most of the rest of the office on one of Easel the weasel's surveillances. When I arrived to the debriefing location most of the office, including Renado and a couple of his guys, were all there. I Hi-5ved Renado and said, "Hay homes, what the hell are you doing here." He responded, "Ah you know, the usual. Customs can't handle a case without us, you know that Dar, Ha, ha. Someone has got to watch out for you Rookies." Weasel briefed everyone that our primary function was to watch this video store for a certain crook to come out of. He gave us a loose description of the crook, and said that we were to follow him upon his departure from the video store. At the end of this briefing I asked weasel why he didn't have a photo of his crook. His response was lame as usual.

We sat there for a couple of hours when Renado drove up to me and said, "Hey Dar, how come we've seen no one coming or going from this store. I mean, is it even open?" I got out of my car and walked past the store. On the front of the door was listed the store hours, and a sign stating that the store was closed. I went back to my car and got the acting supervisor, Robert (Big Bob) Mattivi on the radio. Bob was a rather large fellow, white male, about 53-years-old, and had a heart the size of Wyoming. Bob was also one of the smartest guys that I'd ever met, secondary only to my husband, Ben. I radioed Bob to meet with me, and Renado. By the time Bob arrived, I had already told Renado what I had seen on the door. Renado was laughing mockingly and shaking his head when Bob pulled up.

I briefed Bob and shared my comments about how incredibly stupid Easel was to pull everyone out here on a surveillance of a closed business. I told him how lame it was that he hadn't done any leg work to see when it was opened or have a photo of the crook so that we could maybe do a better job of I.D.ing this guy if he arrived. Renado said, "Bob, where did you get this guy, from the K-Mart school of investigation?" Renado and I busted up laughing. Bob replied, "Hey, this isn't my boy, this is one of Winkowsky's protégés." I stopped laughing, looked at Bob and said, "Bob, buddy, pal, do something about this moron, please. Most of us have real work to do." Bob shook his head, and in an angry tone of voice called Easel over the radio and told him to meet with him. Bob was obviously embarrassed for our agency in front of Renado and members of his agency. Bob apologized and sent us all home. I found it most ironic that as we were leaving and driving past Easel the weasel, Renado pointed out, and yelled to Easel, "Hay everyone, here's the next Customs GS13." I became furious at even the thought that this idiot would be promoted over Ruben or I. This was not the first time that Easel had pulled a bonehead stunt like this, and would receive no consequences from Winkowsky.

Chapter 5

EEO=Frustration

In late February 1997, Ruben asked me if I had filed anything yet. I could sense the concern on his face. I told him of how after several calls and a meeting with Ms. Conales, she still had not provided me with the procedure for filing a class EEO complaint. Ruben then instructed me That there was a timeline. If I didn't file my complaint within 45 days, that I would be ineligible to file. This was the first time that anyone had informed me of time lines.

On March 17, 1997, I filed the following individual EEO complaint. I faxed it to the head of EEO, Lindsey Watts, in Washington D.C., as well as Ms. Conales.

Dear Ms. Watts,

I am filing this Equal Opportunity complaint with great sadness. I feel that I have exhausted all other means to avoid any kind of formal complaint, to include using my chain-of-command. I feel that these issues could be resolved informally with proper communication, development of a truly objective/impartial promotion system, and good personnel training for our management.

For the past eight years, my management has treated me very differently from several of my white, male counterparts. This treatment includes management failing to recommend me for awards on successful cases I have completed, when others are consistently submitted for awards for very similar, and sometimes less results. In addition to awards, these same individuals are consistently supported on their cases, and assignments. I feel that this bias behavior of our management also had an effect on the recent GS-13 promotions at our RAC office.

In August 1996, I talked to our Resident Agent in Charge (RAC) James Wilson about my concerns. As an example of this unfair treatment, I brought to Mr. Wilson's attention one specific case that I put a lot of effort into (Operation Truck Stop) where I was left out completely by my supervisor, Ivan Winkowsky, when awards were presented. Individuals who did much less work on this case than I were presented awards in front of the entire SAC Office. The case agent himself, Robert Mattivi, even fully agreed that the way I was treated was a "real slap in the face." Mr. Wilson agreed that what took place in regards to this case was a mistake and he apologized. After my conversation with Mr. Wilson, the unfair treatment from management subsided for a while. Mr. Wilson retired in December 1994. After Mr. Wilson left, the unfair treatment slowly resumed. In November 1995, another female agent in our office, Millie Landon, complained about very similar issues of gender bias to a member of a Headquarters Inspection Team, named Darcy Fields. Millie's supervisor at the time was Allen Casey. As a result of her complaint, she was treated very badly by Mr. Casey.

This blatant retaliation received by my fellow agent, combined with my own concerns about the way I was being treated prompted me to talk to Mr. Antonio

Pulaski. Mr. Pulaski was, at the time, the ASAIC (Assistant Special Agent In Charge) of the RAIC (Resident Agent In Charge) offices in our area. I told Mr. Pulaski about the concerns of myself, and several other people in our office. I gave him specific examples of unfair treatment where management was engaging in very bias behavior in the areas of awards, schools, and general support on cases. I also warned him that someone would eventually file some type of formal grievance. After my talk with Mr. Pulaski the unfair behavior exhibited by our supervisors stopped. Several months later, Mr. Pulaski left the U.S. Customs service, and again, the unfair behavior of our management resumed.

In November 1996, Special Agent Ruben Sandoval, RAIC/Riverside, filed an EEO complaint regarding many of the same issues and concerns that I am present-ing to you. Through the course of his EEO investigation, I was interviewed by EEO Counselor Victor Ross, San Diego Region and by EEO Supervisor Mary Conales, Los Angeles, Region. I gave Mrs. Conales and Mr. Ross many specific examples of the bias behavior exhibited by our management at RAC/Riverside.

In addition to many other concerns, I explained to them how my promotion score received by the CAAPS promotion system was much higher than my male counterparts who were promoted over me. I explained to Mr. Ross and Mrs. Conales that during the promotion board convened at the SAC office, I gave very clear infor-mation to verify that my score was correct. My board consisted of Mr. Donald Chin, Ms. Kelley Lambert, and Mr. Dudley O'Shea. For each case discussed, not only did I give them the seizure and arrest information requested, I also provided them with names of prosecutors, DEA supervisors, and other agency case agents who would verify all of my work. I had this information written down on a piece of paper next to the correlating case, and I handed the paper to Mr. Chin. Mr. Chin attempted to give this back to me, and I told him that he could keep it. His lack of interest in verifying my work concerned me greatly.

I further explained to Mr. Ross and Mrs. Conales that when the promotion list was released, I telephonically contacted every single person (prosecutors, DEA personnel, case agents) that I had given it in support of my casework. None of them had been contacted by anyone from Customs regarding my cases. This demonstrated to me a lack of verification of casework.

I gave Mrs. Conales and Mr. Ross many other examples of bias/unfair behavior exhibited by our management. I also gave Mrs. Conales a copy of an E-mail message sent to our office for Ivan Winkowsky to post, and he did. The message was from Donald Chin, and directed that any complaints that individuals have at RAIC/Riverside should be forwarded through the chain-of-command. This message was in response to Ruben Sandoval's EEO complaint.

I have a real problem with this message. First of all, you will find that no one tried harder to get cooperation From my chain-of-command regarding these concerns than me. I come from a military background, and I truly believe in the chain of command. This is why I put up with being treated very unfairly for eight (8) years while I continually attempted to obtain help from my chain-of-command. I wanted very much for this to be resolved informally, and made every effort to do so. I went to my supervisor, face to face, and told him of my concerns. When that didn't work, I talked to my RAIC, Mr. Wilson. I subsequently asked for help from ASAIC, Mr. Pulaski. That is, BY DEFINITION, using my chain-of-command!

The combination of my attempting to get help from my chain-of-command, and other individuals complaining to the inspection team about management's behavior should have sparked some type of reaction or show of concern from management. This chain-of-command was the most warned group of people probably in the history of Customs. Most people in our office will tell you that you could see these complaints coming a mile away, and that it could have been easily prevented. I am also aware of other offices where similar grievances have been filed (e.g. Calexico, CA).

In spite of the above concerns, I truly am proud of being a Customs Agent. It amazes me that when it comes to other programs/systems in our agency (i.e. Customs computer programs, laboratories, fitness programs), Customs literally runs circles around every other agency. We have the bragging rights about virtually everything in comparison to our fellow state and federal agencies, except when it comes to systems involving our promotions and awards. When it comes to this, we seem to fall on our face. This agency deserves to have the absolute best promotion and awards system possible.

In light of the recent barrage of complaints involving the recent promotions, the Customs service should accept the fact that what we have just isn't working. We should view this as a learning experience, and as a problem that simply needs to be solved. The CAAPS Scoring System was definitely a step in the right direction, and a good one at that. It just seems to me that in many cases, local management simply tossed this scoring system right out the window, gave it no credence, and reverted back to their old ways.

We do not have to "reinvent the wheel" here to come up with a better system. There are many promotion and awards systems that are excellent models that could be easily tailored to our agency. I DO NOT want this complaint to simply be a part of the problem. I want very much to be a part of the solution. Instead of reacting to these grievances with a "Knee Jerk" overreaction, and/or trying to put a Band-Aid on a great gaping, oozing-hole, let's solve the problem. We can do this, I know we can. Any agency that can come up with amazing systems like our computer system, that other agencies truly are jealous of, can certainly come up with a system of promotion and awards that we can also brag about.

This is the point of my complaint. I'm not asking for people to be punished, let's train them instead. I am, however, pleading with Customs service to take a close look at what we have, and come up with better systems of promotion and awards that we can truly be proud of. When it comes to these issues, there is a severe morale problem among our agents. I am confident that if Customs completed a nation-wide, confidential survey rating of promotional and awards systems, we would be very depressed at the results.

As I reread these words I realize just how naive I really was as to how this system really works, and what the results of this complaint would be. The EEO counselor assigned to me by Mary Conales was SA Tam Zodo assigned to the SAC/Los Angeles, California, and working for Drake Brinkley. SA Zodo had just been promoted under the same promotion system that I was complaining about.

NOTE: I later found out from my attorney that I should have never been assigned an EEO counselor from the same chain-of-command that I was complaining against, and certainly not a white male who was just promoted under that same system that I was beefing.

Several months went by, and SA Zodo never interviewed me. I called numerous times, and talked to him twice. Both times he stated, "Yeah, I'll have to get out there and have you sign some paperwork," but he never showed. Eight months later, and to the shock and dismay of most, we would learn that SA Zodo would be convicted of shop lifting, fraud, violation of federal firearm laws, and money laundering. No wonder he was too busy to interview me. This is the type of agent that Brinkley promoted over Ruben and I.

Chapter 6

The BQL (best qualified list) and EEO: Acronyms With NO Ethics.

On September 17, 1997, Ruben and I were again up for promotion. Winkowsky was tasked by RAIC/Evantie to supervise, review, and verify all case experience regarding the forth-coming GS-13 promotions. RAIC/Evantie was our new Residence office manager for the RAIC/Riverside. Evantie was a tall, skinny, nerdy, white male with dark greasy hair and glasses. Before Evantie arrived, several of us in the office had heard about what an arrogant moron this guy was. He had come from another agency, and basically been promoted through Brinkley's crony, good old boy system. Evantie, like most Customs managers, was well connected to the "Brinkley Brown Noser Gang," and had very little successful cases under his belt. I personally talked to several of his peers, and subordinates from Arizona, and they all said the same thing; that Evantie was an extreme narcissistic jerk, who got into management the normal Customs way. Evantie and Winkowsky were cut from the same mediocre government cloth.

As a result of Winkowsky's review, points would be decided by him and forwarded to the Office of Personnel Management (OPM). Needless to say, I had my reservations about Winkowsky's ability to be unbiased and objective. I wrote a memo to RAIC/Evantie requesting that Winkowsky not be allowed to evaluate the experience of Ruben and I, for obvious reasons. My request was denied. Of course Winkowsky, once again, hammered us on our CAAPS scores, and we still made the

BQL (best qualified list). My previous CAAPS score, and a subsequent CAAPS score both completed by supervisors other than Winkowsky, were 10 points higher than this one that Winkowsky did. Now this is a no-brainer.

On June 3, 1997, I confronted my supervisor Winkowsky about the vehicle assignment situation. This occurred in a parking lot while on surveillance, with SSA/Jerry Johnston witnessing this conversation. At this time I had been driving a car, that for several weeks prior to this date was overheating and dying on me. The car had over 125 thousand miles, and the air conditioning wasn't working. NOTE: these surveillances or controlled deliveries often times began in Indio, California (desert) or there about, in very high temperatures during the months of June and July.

I noticed on this surveillance that Jerry was driving a new car. Jerry's previous vehicle only had 94 thousand miles, wasn't dying, wasn't overheating, had air conditioning, and to my knowledge was in good operating order. When I asked Mr. Winkowsky why was Jerry given a new vehicle when I was clearly the one that needed a different vehicle, Mr. Winkowsky stated, "Mr. Brinkley directed that Jerry's truck be turned in and that Jerry was to be assigned the new vehicle."

I later asked Jerry about this, and he stated that, "All I know is that Brinkley ordered it." When I confronted Jerry with this I could tell that he felt bad for me, and didn't want me to be mad at him over it. I assured him that I knew that this was not of his doing, and that everything was cool. Jerry was a soft-spoken, handsome, white male, dark hair, dark eyes, which had that distinctive, ultra-professional, military orah about him. Jerry and I were sort of kindred spirits. We were the only agents in the office that were prior military officers. He believed as I did, as we were both taught, that the mission comes first, then your men, and last your self. We were both later to find that this was not the philosophy of the Department of Treasury. Nonetheless, Jerry Johnston was a good man, and an excellent criminal investigator. That was June 1997, and in November 1997 the blue utility truck that was supposedly ordered by Mr. Brinkley to be turned in (the excuse for me to continue for several weeks to operate an unsafe vehicle) is currently being operated by Ruben Sandoval, as documented by the vehicle maintenance sheet.

On June 6, 1997, I walked into the office. Winkowsky stopped me in the hall and motioned that I come into the office of Yolanda Rios, our Office Administrator. Yolanda Rios was a dark-skinned, short haired, very pretty, Puerto Rican woman. Yolanda's demeanor was very direct, foreword, and very outspoken. She had a great since of humor, and when she talked she always talked with her hands. Yolanda was a real kick in the pants, and made work a fun place for everyone. When Winkowsky stopped me in the hall he seemed very nervous, and had a "slippery" demeanor about him. He told me that there was an EEO investigator here to interview people regarding Ruben Sandoval's case. Just minutes before I was to be interviewed by Mr. Orlando Lopez, Winkowsky told me that new cars were coming into the SAC office and that I would be getting one. I couldn't believe what I was hearing. This jerk was attempting to soften up my testimony by bribing me with a car. I shook my head in condescension and disgust. I said in a distrustful tone of voice, "sure Ivan, sure." What little respect that I had for that man just disintegrated. I was surprised at his fear and willingness to sink so low. This angered me. I went into the meeting with Orlando Lopez, and told the truth, pulling no punches, especially on Winkowsky's behalf.

On August 5, 1997, I contacted Mary Conales and complained about the EEO counselor that she assigned me. She immediately assigned me a new EEO counselor, Senior Inspector, Anna Francisco. August 97 was the first time that I actually met with an EEO counselor. I asked around about Anna, and the feedback that I got was very good. She was perceived as a very good inspector, and well respected as an EEO counselor. I met with Anna at our RAC office. She explained to me about my EEO rights, and explained about the timelines. She even had an EEO rights form that she filled out for me, that explained to me about my EEO rights. As she was doing this, I wondered why Mary Conales failed to advise me of any of this.

On December 12, 1997, I gave Anna Francisco all of my documentation that she had given to me to date. This documentation included a sworn statement written by SA Sandy Nunn in support of both Ruben and myself. Sandy Nunn and I had been friends since we first entered Customs over 10 years ago. Sandy was this cute, tiny, little blond woman, who had a real spark of life in her eyes. When I first met Sandy we became fast friends. We both were these petite, shorthaired; Blondie girls, and we were often endearingly referred to as the "Glitter Girls." This nickname had as much to do with our wardrobes as it did anything else. Sandy and I were known to dress a lot more up-scale than the average agent. We were both clothes hounds. My husband often referred to us as the "Emelda Marcos's" of federal agents. Between the two of us, we could fill up a warehouse of shoes and clothes. Sandy was assigned to the SAIC/LA office, and was a brilliant agent. She was the case agent on the very famous "L.A. Jewelry Mart Case." This case was a huge international money laundering case, was written up in Newsweek, and was one of Customs most successful cases ever. Sandy was no slouch as an agent, and I had tremendous respect for her.

When Sandy offered this statement to me and I read it, I was very impressed. I told her of the concerns that I had regarding the impending doom that I felt would follow as the result of this statement. I told her that this was really going to piss Brinkley off, and warned her to be ready to accept the consequences of a possible transfer. She bravely plowed forward, in disbelief of my prediction. I was very proud of her. The following is the professional, eloquent, and truthful statement written by Sandy Nunn:

> Since October 1988, I have been employed with the
> U.S. Customs Service in Los Angeles, California in the

capacity of a Special Agent. During this 9-year period, I have been assigned to the Office of the Special Agent in Charge located on Terminal Island. As a long-standing employee in this office, I have had the opportunity to actively observe the overall morale, conduct, general health and well-being of the employee base, daily happenings, politics, and so forth of all personnel assigned to this office. This has afforded me the unique position to draw certain comparisons with regard to each of the five (5) areas outlined above.

When I arrived at the SAC/Los Angeles in October 1988, I observed that employee morale was extremely high. Employees were happy, enthusiastic about their work, motivated, and felt very relaxed in their dealings with upper management. I observed during that time that management appeared to care a great deal about the employees as individuals and that an "open door policy" was encouraged to make it easier for employees to address concerns. This attitude made employees feel more comfortable. Subsequently, for the most part, employee health and well being appeared to be very optimum since stress levels were low. As a result of a positive work atmosphere, productivity was at an all-time high.

Contrasting that picture with the SAC/Los Angeles today, I observe an office in which employee morale is dangerously low, happiness is non-existent, enthusiasm and motivation has been severely curbed contributing to low productivity levels, and stress has replaced relaxed feelings to the degree that several agents have had to go out on stress leave or have had to resort to taking anti-depressant medications such as

Prozac. Further, U.S. Customs is losing experienced agents who feel they have no choice but to leave early either through early retirement or by switching agencies. I have also observed an onslaught of stress-related disorders among my fellow agents consisting of headaches, inability to eat or sleep, feelings of frustration and anger, even suicidal thoughts. Further exacerbating the problem is what I perceive as a strong tendency on the part of management to micromanage the work of the agents of this office by engaging in lengthy case review meetings, playing definite favorites with certain agent personnel to the exclusion of others with regard to how cases and/or other assignments are to be divided and carried out, and by engaging in favoritism with regard to promotions. Most significant of all is an attitude by management, which I would term "management by threat." There is a definite attitude by management of this office that the way to keep the agents under control is to threaten and intimidate them into submission. This is very common knowledge among everyone in this office and it takes place very openly and to such degree that I have actually witnessed personality changes in agents I have worked with for many years. Further, agents who I know to be highly competent and mature have actually openly expressed feelings of fear toward management. This is due to the fact that there are many examples of productive agents who have been intimidated, threatened, and harassed by upper management over a period of time in this office, as well as throughout the entire Customs Service. Coming from a highly educated background in the field of electronics engineering and

having served in the corporate world prior to my
employment with U.S. Customs, I find this management style very inappropriate and highly contributory
to what is termed under law as a hostile working envi-
ronment. In point of fact, this behavior is illegal under
federal laws and should not be tolerated.

Therefore, I am making this statement of my own free
will based upon my observations into these matters.
Further, by making this statement and signing my complete name, I am hereby designating myself as a
"whistleblower" as defined under the Whistleblower Act
with all the protections accorded me under this law.

SANDRA G. NUNN
Special Agent
U.S. Customs Service

On January 8, 1998, when Anna Francisco finished her EEO investigation, she put her report, which included Sandy's statement, on the
desk of EEO supervisor Mary Conales. On January 12, 1998, Drake
Brinkley signed a memo ordering that Sandy Nunn be transferred.
Sandy called me and explained what had happened. She was pissed off
and on the verge of tears. When Sandy's boss called her into his office
to break the news to her, he told her that he had just found out. Sandy
was being transferred to the DEA, technical task force, in downtown
Los Angeles. In our agency, this was commonly referred to as the
dumping ground. Everyone knew that this is where management
sends all the people they perceive as "problem children." When Sandy
walked out of her supervisor's office, she saw the Customs Task force
coordinator Fred Lauder walking out of the weekly office management meeting. When he entered the hall she walked up to him and
stated, "Hi, I hear that I'm going to be working for you starting next

week." Fred Lauder was completely surprised by this. He had no idea that Sandy was being transferred to his group. We found this most interesting. This is not how normal transfers work. Supervisors are always advised well in advanced of any personnel changes being made. Two days after SAC Brinkley signed the transfer memo for Sandy Nunn, Brinkley signed another memo addressed to all agents at the SAC/LA. This memo stated:

> With the expected influx of new personnel in the next 6 months there is a need to place them where they will be the most effective for the Office of Investigations. In an effort to get a better understanding of the background and experience level of current SAC/LA agents within the immediate commuting distance of Terminal Island, LAX and RAC/OR, please advise me of the following information for each agent within your chain-of-command. Please submit this info on all 1811 personnel to Associate SAC Woody Pillsbury by February 1. Thank you.

> 1. Time as a Customs Special Agent?
> 2. Time in present group/office?
> 3. Time spent in Terminal Island, RAC/LX, and RAC/OR?
> 4. Investigative disciplines worked?
> 5. Office/group in which you would most desire to work within the SAC/LA?
> 6. Would you desire a tour in Headquarters?

> Drake Brinkley

This memo basically allowed all agents of the SAC/LA to have input on where and if they would like to be transferred, everyone, that is, except Sandy Nunn. Sandy's transfer memo was obvious a knee-jerk reaction to something, and the something was obviously Sandy's letter that was supposed to be kept anonymous. The only way that management could have known about this was from Mary Conales. If Mary Conales leaked this information to management, then this would be a clear violation of Sandy Nunn's rights, and a violation of the Privacy Act, and Whistleblower Act. I knew it with all my being that bitch Conales had given us up.

I called Anna Francisco and told her what was going on with Sandy. She was pissed off, and very concerned. Anna later confronted Conales about the situation, and Conales conveniently fired Anna from being an EEO counselor. All of my suspicions about Conales being a snake, in bed with management, were confirmed. Anna was devastated. She called me up to give me this news, and she started crying. I began to hate Mary Conales. Sandy filed an EEO retaliation complaint based upon the aforementioned.

On March 2, 1998, Mary Conales lied in a sworn statement that alleged that in our December 1996 meeting at her office in Long Beach, I didn't request counseling on particular issues affecting me, and that Ms. Conales made me aware of what the EEO process entailed. When I read this I was furious. What a crock of shit. What did she think that I drove 3 hours one-way to her office for, to have lunch? Subsequent to this, my EEO complaint was denied by the Regional Complaint Center, based on timeliness. Oh how convenient! This witch strung me along, not notifying me of any timelines, and built in a standard excuse for my complaint to be denied. I later learned that this was a routine tactic of hers, stringing people along, not telling them of timelines, and lying about it later. She did this to Ervin Rios, Ruben, Sandy, and numerous others, too many to mention. There was a definite, well-documented pattern here, if only someone cared enough to look. But of course, no one would. Conales was completely in bed with Customs management.

On March 26, 1998, Sandy and I met with Jay Rosden, Port Director, Lukeville, AZ. The purpose of this meeting was for Sandy to file an EEO retaliation report for her forced transfer. I arrived at the Lobby of the Hilton at approximately 10:30am and met with Mr. Rosden. It was approximately 30 minutes later when Special Agent Sandy Nunn arrived. Our interviews were still ongoing when at approximately 1500hrs I got a page from my acting Group Supervisor, David Gray. David Gray was another very nerdy, unattractive, balding, white male. He was a complete computer geek, complete with pocket protector and wire-rimmed glasses. When I telephoned Gray back he asked me where I was and what I was doing. His voice sounded stressed, and direct. I asked him if he got my voice mail messages or not, and he said that he did. He then told me that Lawrence (Evantie), wanted to know what was going on. I answered back that this was regarding my EEO issue. Then David, in a weak attempt at intimidation stated, "well what issue, I mean is this something new or what." I replied, "Well why don't you speak to the EEO Counselor yourself," and I handed the phone to Mr. Rosden.

As I handed the phone to Mr. Rosden, he had a look of "oh shit" on his face. I felt a sense of guilt about passing the buck to Mr. Rosden in order to evade being further grilled, and to get out of this very inappropriate situation. Mr. Rosden seemed like a real great guy, and a good supervisor, something not common to Customs. Mr. Rosden got on the phone and at first it was clear that he was talking to David Gray. Then the conversation changed and I could tell that Mr. Rosden was now talking to RAIC Lawrence Evantie by the use of Lawrence's name. At the very beginning of this conversation SA Arnold Connez, SAC/LA walked up to us in the lobby, and also witnessed the conversation. It was very apparent to everyone that Mr. Rosden was being "interrogated" by Lawrence Evantie. It was clear to everyone that Mr. Rosden was attempting to be polite, yet evasive to Evantie's questions, and was feeling extremely, uncomfortable about the situation he was in. The poor man was squirming. Sandy and I had not yet filed out any paperwork or had the opportunity to inform Mr. Rosden whether or not we wanted to remain anonymous regarding this issue.

When Mr. Rosden got off of the phone, the look on his face was one of disbelief. He told us that he was very uncomfortable about the way that was handled. I told him that I thought that was very inappropriate, and could have been perceived as intimidating. He agreed. We finished our interviews at approximately 1700hrs. I knew traffic would be a pain, due to the rain and rush hour, so I decided to wait out the traffic and have something to eat. We were all hungry. I departed for home at approximately 1900hrs.

As I was driving up the street to my house (approximately 2100hrs), I got a page from Dave Gray at our office in Riverside. I went into the house and called him back. Dave started the conversation by attempting to put me on the speakerphone. This pissed me off. The nerve of this rat bastered. I was convinced that he was doing that because he wanted another person who was there to listen to our conversation, and that person was probably Evantie. He tried several times to engage the speakerphone but he couldn't get it to work. I thought, you stupid fool, you don't even know how to use the speaker device on the phone. Yeah that's an IA agent for you. At no time did Gray have the common courtesy to ask me if it was okay to put me on the speakerphone or allow someone else to listen to our conversation. I was livid.

Gray started telling me that the purpose for his call was to see if I was all right. I thought to myself, bullcrap! Then he began asking me questions like why are you just getting home right now, and why did it take so long. I explained to the dunce that because of the rain, it took me three hours to get from my house to Long Beach this morning, and that the interviews just lasted longer than we thought. I further explained that I didn't want to fight rush hour traffic coming back, so I stayed to eat, and that I left Long Beach at about 1900hrs and was just arriving home when he paged.

Then Gray stated that he just wanted me to know what happened today with the phone call with Evantie and everything. He stated, "Lawrence just wanted to know what was going on, and why you were gone so long." Gray further explained in an official tone of voice as though he was performing for someone, "that the EEO counselor should have contacted Riverside management and made arrangements to conduct the interviews at the RAC/Riverside Office, and that the EEO counselor was incorrect by not doing so." I responded by telling Gray, "I feel that what took place on the phone with Evantie "grilling" the EEO Counselor was very inappropriate." Gray said, "Lawrence has every right to know that information, and that it wasn't inappropriate." We politely argued the point, as if both of us feared that we were being recorded or watched, and I then informed Gray that there were three people who were present and witnessed this conversation between the EEO counselor and Lawrence Evantie. There was dead silence, and you could feel Gray's sphincter puckering up from the other side of the phone. I told Gray, "That's right Gray, all three people witnessed Evantie's inquisition of Mr. Rosden, and it was very inappropriate."

I told Gray that even Mr. Rosden told us that he was very uncomfortable about that conversation, and that he agreed with me that it was inappropriate. Gray responded that the EEO counselor should have never stated that to me, and that the EEO counselor would be in very big trouble with his management if they knew that he said that. I stated that the EEO counselor didn't need to tell us how uncomfortable he was, it was painfully obvious that the man was almost squirming, and that we all saw the obvious for ourselves. I reiterated my position to Gray, that I felt it was an inappropriate way to handle things. Then Gray changed the topic back to the reason for this phone call was just to make sure that I was okay and that I made it home safe. This was such a joke. In 11 years of being an agent, going out on surveillance and deals where

I returned in the middle of the night, no one in Customs had ever called to see if I got home okay, NO ONE.

After I hung up with Gray, I again felt that I was being inappropriately contacted by management, and that if management had a problem with the way that Mr. Rosden was conducting himself, then Gray and Evantie should have been on the phone to Mr. Rosden expressing these views, not on the phone at 2100hrs with me. I knew that the real purpose of the 2100hrs phone call from but kisser Gray, was just another fishing expedition about this EEO matter that at this point was none of his business. Gray was just doing Evantie's dirty work for him.

After my conversation with Gray, my phone rang and it was Sandy. I told her what had just happened and suggested that we call Mr. Rosden. Sandy placed a three-way call to Mr. Rosden. I told Mr. Rosden what had just transpired, and what Gray had said about him being in trouble. I apologized to Mr. Rosden if I had gotten him into any trouble, and he assured me that everything was all right. I further explained of how I felt that both of these telephone conversations were totally inappropriate. I explained to him that I thought it was bullcrap that I was placed in the middle between the EEO counselor and management's opinion of the way the EEO counselor should conduct his business, and he agreed. Sandy and I were both livid. I had a hard time sleeping that night, and had a feeling of something odious about to happen. My stomach burned.

Chapter 7

Operation "Railroad" Begins

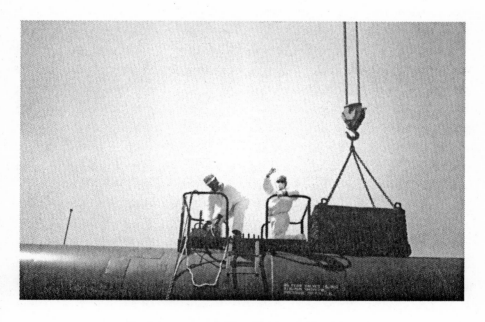

Darlene on top of rail tanker car with seizure

On April 7, 1998, Gray called me into his office. He asked me if I still had my rail project up and running. I told him yes. He told me that he had just taken a call from inspectors at Calexico. Four days ago they had sent a series of tanker cars to Union Pacific to be weighed, and that they'd be up next week to check them. I said, "next week, we will loose border search authority if we wait that long. Those idiots don't know what they are doing." Gray said, "Can you handle it?" and handed me the note. I could sense concern in Gray's demeanor. Gray and I go way back. We used to be very close confidants. Then Gray joined IA and changed. Gray was concerned because I had been fighting some sort of bug for several months now. I was struggling with this because I had also began my training for the 1999 Police Olympics, and for the past couple of days, I was running a low grade fever, having troubles breathing, and losing my voice.

I grabbed the note, and as I was walking back to my office, Gray laughed and said "Choo, choooo." This was a reminder of a prior embarrassment involving a tanker car caper that everyone commonly referred to as the "Geraldo Rivera Tanker Car Caper"(reference to when News Caster/Talk Show Host, Geraldo Rivera opened that tomb of that mobster on national T.V., and it was empty). I ignored Gray, placed it out of my mind, and pushed a call to my contact with the Union Pacific (UP) Rail Police, Special Agent Tom Best. Tom Best and I had been working together for about six years or so, off and on, on rail projects. Tom was a great old guy who knew more about the railroad than anyone I'd ever met. He was an older white male, big smile, bald head, and reminded me of this picture of a railroad conductor I had seen On the cover of a children's book. If you put Tom in a conductor's hat, and a pair of overalls, he'd be a dead ringer for that picture. I asked Tom about the cars, and he responded in a disgusted tone of voice, "Yeah, there here, all 20 of them, clogging up my yard. Can you help me out with this Darlene?" I told him that I was on my way.

As I drove over there I couldn't help thinking about that embarrassing episode that Gray was "choo chooing" at me over. I remembered that about five years back, I pegged a car as suspicious because of the way it was imported, and the shenanigans that had taken place at the Calexico, California port of entry, where the Customs hold was released. From Calexico, it traveled to Colton, California prior to when I had arranged for it. This put the car in the rail yard on New Years Eve. In addition, on the trip up from Calexico, the rail car became unaccounted for, for about nine to 12 hours. No body could figure out where it had been in this missing time frame. I was duty agent that night, and had already gotten a call from my comrade, Ervin Rios, on a suspected load of opium coming through Ontario Airport, UPS (United Parcel Service). I was at UPS, attempting to arrange for a controlled delivery of the seizure to Redding, California, when I got the call from Tom Best. Best started off the conversation with, "Do you know where your rail car is?" in a coy tone of voice. I said, "Why Best, you gonna tell me that it ain't sitting where it's supposed to be." Best said, "no, it's heerrreee" (singing it like that kid on that movie Poltergeist).

I had my hands full trying to arrange with Customs Agents out of San Francisco, a controlled delivery of the opium. It was a hard task since the agents would rather ring in the New Year with a party than with casework. I ended up making arrangements with State BNE (Bureau of Narcotics Enforcement) instead of my own agency for the controlled delivery. Ed Saite, head of security with UPS, let us deliver the package on one of his planes.

I had time before the UPS crew and I left on the controlled delivery, so I met Best over at the rail yard. Sure enough, here was our car sitting there. Best made arrangements for the car to be weighed, and to be placed on a bad order (routed to a side track where cars go for repair) so that it would stay put until I could deal with it the next day.

I pulled another all-nighter on yet another controlled delivery that Ervin Rios (no relationship to Yolanda Rios, Riverside Investigative Aid) had made of seized opium. Ervin Rios was a Latin Male of average height and weight, who was anything but average when it came to the job. The man was brilliant, and stacked up seizures one after another. I donned a UPS uniform, flew to Redding, and delivered the package. We ended up seizing 18 lbs of opium and arresting two guys. It made the papers up there as a record seizure of opium.

The next day I started tackling the logistical nightmare of dealing with this tanker car. I got about three hours of sleep, sucked down an ocean of coffee and Mountain Dew, and headed over to the rail yard. When I walked into the UP Police station, Best was sitting there laughing his but off. I knew that this wasn't good. I said, "O.K. Best, where is it now?" Best responded, "The real question you should be asking is how did it get there." The car was on an out bound, about to exit the yard. Thank God Best caught it. Best said that the UP computer system (the Eddie Star System) showed that someone from Customs had released the hold. I chalked it up to stupidity, and laziness. Not all inspectors were of the Caliber as Ervin Rios. Little did I know what I had stumbled into.

We arranged for the car to be moved to the GATX (General American Tanker Car Company) facility, about a mile away, so that it could be safely entered. On the following Tuesday, we started bleeding it out (burning off the excess fuel from the bottom of the car) in preparation for safely opening the car. For safety purposes, we have to notify the fire department when we crack open these cars, for fear of possible booby traps (crooks are known to booby trap large loads of narcotics to keep them from getting ripped off). Some idiot from the fire department leaked it to the press. On Tuesday, the hill overlooking the GATX yard was full of media. Needless to say, when we cracked it open, it was empty. I felt just like Geraldo Rivera when he opened the Mafia's tomb in front of the world on national TV, only to find nothing. For weeks after this, everyone would make choo choo noises when they walked past me, and call me Geraldo. As I relived this unfortunate memory, I couldn't help but laugh.

On the way to the yard, I called Renado (Sgt. Detective prior narcotics, and head of San Bernardino P.D's Intelligence Section) for some help with a narcotics dog. As soon as I mentioned a rail car, Renado started laughing, and saying choo choo. I said, "Ha, Ha, real funny you butt head, now get your fanny over here and find me a dog and this time Einstein, find me a real dog, not just some stray that you picked up from the pound." On the last embarrassing tanker car episode, Ranado supplied a stupid dog that alerted himself almost to death over an empty car.

When I got there, Best had already placed the car on a bad order (the computer listing of the placement of damaged rail cars) and had the haz-matt (hazardous materials) folks there. Dennis Bar with UP haz-matt, Edmundo the foreman from GATX, and Ervin Rios were already there. I climbed on top with my cutting sheers, and removed the Customs seal on the man-way hatch cover. I bagged and tagged the seal for evidence. Edmundo and Bar lifted the hatch cover, and exposed the bolts to the hatch-port containing the pressure valves. We immediately noticed that the bolts holding on the hatch-port were hand painted white, like with an artist's paintbrush. I looked down at Ervin and said, "What the hell!" I motioned with my head for Ervin to climb on top. Ervin sighed as he didn't like climbing on top of these things, but he came up anyway. None of us had ever seen this type of painting before. It was not consistent with normal shop style painting. I smiled at Ervin, and we both smiled at Best. I said to Edmundo and Bar, "Lets pressure test it."

At my request, they moved the car to another location, out of sight of any public or media. I was determined not to have another Gerardo Rivera episode. As we began the pressure test, we got yet another surprise, negative pressure. When we opened the valve, we heard a distinct sucking sound, and no air exited or registered on the outside gage for several minutes. This car had been vacuumed sealed. There was no legitimate, commercial purpose for vacuum sealing one of these pressurized tanker cars; in fact, it creates a safety hazard if the car is loaded with certain volatile commodities. About this time, Renado pulled up with a dog. I told Renado what we had, and he immediately became excited. He had the car inspected several times by the narcotics detection dog, and the dog did not alert. I looked at Renado and said, "Another pound puppy Renado." Renado responded, "Kiss my ass, Catalan," and we both laughed.

I made a call to Gray who was acting group supervisor at the time, and told him what we had. He said he was on his way. When Gray arrived, I briefed him on how these cars worked, and why these indicators (bolts painted white, car manifested as empty, port of origin) were so significant. Rios was already working his magic on the Customs Computer system called ACS. ACS was a system that tracked all imports into the country. Rios pulled the entries on this car and brought it to the sight. The car was manifested as a return empty, and had been exported back to the U.S. from a company called Grassa," in Sinnaloa, Mexico. Grassa is Spanish for oil. I asked Best to set the car up to be weighed. I told him to hump it (a term used for the large scales that weigh the cars entering the Colton rail yard; they roll down hill, and gravity carries them over a hump with the scales) at least three times to ensure an accurate read.

It was good to see Ervin again. Ervin had just won a fight against Customs for wrongful firing. He had been off of work for over a year, and had been financially devastated by this. At the time of his firing, Ervin was working at the Los Angeles International Air Port (LAX), and was about to complete a money transport over to the Customs office to place in the vault. His partner was a girl named Sarah Brooks. As Ervin was pulling out of the LAX parking lot in his POV (Privately Owned Vehicle), a carload of "Vatos" (slang for Mexican males) crashed into him. This accident was clearly not Ervin's fault. They all got out of the car, and Ervin attempted to get information from them. None of them would produce any identification, and by their appearance and the appearance of their vehicle, Ervin deduced that they were probable "wet-backs" (slang for illegal aliens). The driver of the other car offered Ervin fifty bucks for the damage, and Ervin took it, knowing that he would never see these guys again. If he didn't take the fifty bucks he'd end up with nothing. When Ervin returned to the Customs office, he briefed his supervisor, and reported the incident to Internal Affairs, via agency policy, a mistake he would later regret.

This type of thing happens a hundred times a day in southern California and numerous times to dozens of Customs Agents. A fender-bender occurs on the freeway with small damage, and cash is passed and accepted in order to avoid insurance increases, No big deal. But, for some unexplained reason, IA went after Ervin like he'd robbed a bank, and fired him for this. No one could believe it. Both Ruben and I testified on Ervin's behalf, and Department of Treasury's grievance system later declared it a wrongful firing and Ervin got his job back. Still, no one from Customs was disciplined in any way for Ervin's wrongful firing. There was no justice or consequence for all of the anguish and hardship dealt to Ervin by Internal Affairs. We were all in disbelief of the whole situation.

It took most of the rest of the day to manipulate the tanker car back through the yard (one of the largest rail yards in the U.S.) and get the damn thing weighed. While this was occurring, Gray was on the phone with the powers that be, begging and pleading for the authorization and funds to pop this thing open. I was on the phone to my favorite AUSA (Assistant United States Attorney), Yvette Palazuelos. Yvette was our federal prosecutor on several of our Title III's (wire tap investigations), while I was on the HIDTA (High Intensity Drug Trafficking Area) Group 50, task force. I really admired Yvette. Yvette was a cute, tiny, Latino woman, even smaller than me, and a real go-getter. She reminded me of Mighty Mouse. I briefed her on what we had on the case so far and of the time that had expired. I had pulled from the UP (Union Pacific) computer the rout that the car had taken and could articulate to her a good, extended border search. She agreed and granted me extended border search authority (authority only granted to U.S. Customs which authorized searches of people, possessions, vehicles, and commodities entering the U.S.).

The tanker car weighed in at almost 9 thousand lbs, which was over the manufacturers scheduled lightweight for this type of pressurized car. Gray via telephone, authorized me to have the car moved to the GATX facility, while we waited for authorization to pop it open. Gray and I were now convinced that the car was probably loaded. Up pulled Gray, and Evantie and I briefed him. I suggested that from this point on, in order to maintain good border search authority and to provide security, we should have the tanker car guarded until it is opened. Gray agreed, and told me that it was probably going to be tomorrow afternoon before they got authorization/funding to open it. This was okay as it was probably going to take several hours to move it to the GATX facility anyway. I made it clear to Edmundo (GATX foreman) that I wanted this thing out of sight of the public and the media. I reminded him of the last "Geraldo Rivera" episode. I didn't want a repeat performance.

Chapter 8

The Dream

That night I sat in my G-ride (slang for government issued vehicle) baby-sitting the tanker car. I missed tucking in my kids again and longed to hold them, kiss them, and hear their cute little voices tell me all about their day. I called them on the phone, spoke to each of them, and hugged and kissed them on the phone, but it wasn't the same. I envied my husband Ben for choosing a more normal career in private industry. I dozed off, and I had the dream again. This would be the 17th time. When I first started having this dream, it scared me to death. I thought it was some type of warning of danger to my kids or something. Now after having it so many times, I was more curious than anything. This time the dream took me back to the house that I grew up in, in Dayton, Kentucky. Each time the dream took me to different places, but the dream would always be the same. I was standing in the street in front of my home. A small boy about two years old was stumbling down the street towards me, crying, shaking, and dirty. I ran to the child and picked him up, holding him tight, while I took him into the house and began to bath him. I tried to get him to talk to me, but he wouldn't. This child was so beautiful; he had eyes like the ocean that looked right through me. As I began washing him, I noticed that the filth wouldn't come off. I kept trying to get the grime off, but it wouldn't come. The more I tried the more despairing and heart-broken I became. The child just stared at me as if he were begging with his eyes for me to help him. His eyes teared and I felt like I was dying inside because I couldn't separate him from the filth.

Just then a loud crash startled me awake, and I went for my gun. I realized it was just the rail cars bumping together as they were being hooked up. My rapid breathing slowed, and I secured my firearm. I then realized that I had the dream again, and I began to worry if it had any meaning, or if I was simply loosing my mind. I had three hours left on my shift and just wanted to go home to my family. I thought of the millions of times that I was so tired that I wanted to resign and just go home. But I was afraid that I couldn't make it as a regular person. Being a criminal investigator was all I knew. That had been my whole world all of my adult life. As a child I dreamed of being an undercover police woman as I watched Charlie's Angels. Who was I if I wasn't a federal agent. I was sure that the courage to make it in some other industry/profession was lacking within me. Still, this dream is becoming more frequent, more haunting, and raising my curiosity about dreams to new levels.

Chapter 9

The Load

It ended up taking two days to bleed out the fumes and clear the tanker car with haz-mat. Then the haz-mat guys, Gray and Ruben Sandoval all conspired that I should be the one to make the entry. So, they suited me up in this haz-mat costume, which made me look like an astronaut. I really didn't want to do this. I was still sick and running a fever, and my ears had been ringing for a couple of weeks. When they turned on the oxygen in my mask, I knew that the mix was too rich, but the moron rigging me up wouldn't listen. They rigged a tri-pod on top of the car, and lowered me down through the man-way port on a rope. It was pitch dark inside, and I was trying to hold a spotlight and a video camera. As I was being lowered through the man-way, I cracked my helmet on the edge, and the helmet fell to the bottom. I remember feeling light headed and giggling about the whole thing. I was certain that the oxygen mix was too rich, and didn't give a damn. As I was being lowered, I could see large packages piled up at both ends, and lots of them. I was so stoked; I knew we had a load and a big one. As I reached the bottom, I was stumbling around tripping over packages of weed and cocaine. I was trying to video the contents of the car, and dropped my light. It was difficult enough to see with the facemask I had on, and when the light went out it was a pretty clostrafobic moment. I tried to control my breathing, but I felt myself hyperventilating. They had a radio transmitter/receiver in the mask, and I heard Bar yelling, "Hey, are you all right? Are you all right?" I answered "Yes," and told them to get me out. As I reached the top, I felt really woozy and nauseous.

I immediately started tearing at my facemask to get it off. Bar said, "Wow, hold it, hold it, calm down, were getting it off of you." They got my mask off, and I felt like I was on an elevator ride, experiencing that sinking feeling. I also felt very weak and sleepy. Bar examined the O2 regulator and I heard him say, "Well, no wonder you were having problems, they set your O2 too rich for your weight." I looked over at the technician who set my regulator, and with a disdainful smirk on my face I said, "You stupid clown, I told you it was too rich." He gave me an embarrassed look and turned away. All I wanted to do was just lay down there and go to sleep, but I noticed everyone down on the ground watching me, waiting for some type of reaction, so I stood and gave everyone a big thumbs up.

Everyone started high-fiving, and I climbed down off the car. I got out of the suit, and Ruben, Ervin, Jerry Johnston and Renado gave me hugs and congratulations. I told them about how much was in there, and they were pleased. As I sat there trying to regulate my breathing and holding back the appearance of wanting to vomit and pass out, people were walking up and congratulating me. I looked over at Lawrence Evantie, and the bonehead was throwing me mean looks. He walked over and in a condescending tone of voice said, "Well Darlene, are you just going to sit there, or are you going to arrange for a controlled delivery?" He pointed as his watch and said, "the clock's ticking." I looked back at him and mumbled a stream of absurdities under my breath. "You son-of-a-bitch, rat bastered; I thought to myself, you can't stand this, can you?" Then I stood up and replied, "I'll see to it, sir."

I went to the GATX restroom and attempted to barf. I hadn't eaten anything all day, so all that I could manage was the dry heaves. My ears were ringing louder and louder. I splashed water on my face and went back out to the car. I briefed AUSA Yvette and set up the logistics for a controlled delivery to a lumber yard/warehouse on Mill Street in San Bernardino. SSA Bob Mattivi took over carrying out of the logistics of the controlled delivery. Ruben worked with Renado in getting us bodies

Darlene in Hazardous Materials suit ready to make entry into a rail tanker car

for surveillance for the next few days. Gray took over the bagging and tagging of the evidence.

At this point I had been awake for almost 30 hours straight, and Gray, Renado, Ruben, and Mattivi knew that I was fading fast. They were all ordering me to go home and get some rest, so that I could be good for the delivery for tomorrow. I didn't argue with them. The seizure ended up being 8000 pounds of marijuana, and 34 kilos of cocaine. I was so burned out, I didn't feel anything when the told me the amount. I just wanted to go home, but I was so tired, I was afraid to drive home for fear of falling asleep at the wheel. I stopped and got a highly caffenated Mountain Dew and guzzled it down on an empty stomach. It wasn't the best idea I ever had. By the time I got home, my stomach felt like I had a hole burning in it. In an attempt to relieve the acid, I drank some milk and went to look at my kids. They were fast asleep. I kissed them and covered them up. I sat on the floor watching my youngest sleep and drank my milk. He looked so peaceful and beautiful. I wondered, as I often did lately, if I was being a good mother and if I was doing the right thing for them. As I was finally sinking into a deep sleep it hit me; the tanker car wasn't empty. I am not Geraldo Rivera. I am not Geraldo Rivera. I slept well.

0600hrs the following morning (Saturday), I got a call from Gray. He asked me if I was up to starting on the federal anticipatory search warrant. I told Gray, "Gray, I've already got it written in my head." Gray replied, "Well bring your head and your fingers in so that you can type this up." I responded, "No problem." My husband was lying next to me and asked, "Gotta go back to work babe?" I responded, "Sorry, honey." I replied, "we had a big night last night." Ben hugged me, and congratulated me on my seizure. I explained about Evantie, and Ben told me, "He's just mad because you're showing up his boys, and that's not supposed to happen. Just blow him off." As I got up, Ben went down stairs and fixed me breakfast. He saw that I was still sick and yelled at me for not making a doctors appointment. He made me promise to go to the

Seizure of narcotics inside of rail tanker car

Photo of Darlene with large seizure of narcotics taken from rail tanker car

doctor on Monday. As I sat down to eat breakfast with him, I realized just how lucky I was. I wanted to tell him about the dream, but I was afraid of what he would think of me. Again, I kept it to myself.

I worked on the warrant and met with the powers that be with the railroads and San Bernardino Police Department. The office was a buzz with everyone working together to run down leads. The FBI showed up, trying to lay claim to our case. These bunch of morons had nothing, and we had everything, and yet the turf war was on. Typical FBI, wanting you to give them all of your information, yet refusing to share anything of theirs. I got a hold of Yvette, and gave her a heads-up on the impending turf war. She told me not to worry. I had a verbal altercation with the FBI agent who had done some undercover work on the front company (phony private corporation set up to mask illegal activities) that had leased this tanker car. I saw right through the FBI Agent's bullshit and wasn't exactly politically correct with him, so they left.

Chapter 10

The Scare Of My Life

Monday morning, I went to the doctor's again. This was the third time that I had gone in three months, and they still weren't helping me. Due to the ringing in my ears, I was referred to an ears, nose, and throat specialist down the hall. I was given a hearing test and had a blood work done. After all of the tests, the doctor met with me. He told me that he was mildly concerned because I had several symptoms that matched Multiple Sclerosis (MS). When he told me this, my arms, legs and face felt numb, and my chest got tight. He told me that he was scheduling me for an MRI on Thursday afternoon.

I went back to the office in a total daze. I immediately started worrying about my husband and kids, not to mention myself, if I had MS. My stomach started burning as I sat at my desk. I had just sat down when I heard Gray yell for Ruben and I to come into his office. Gray told me that Janet Reno had asked for a daily briefing on my case. It seems that this was the first case involving a controlled delivery of narcotics using a rail car. In a displeased manner, Gray started firing off questions about the FBI's related case. I softly interrupted him with the news that I had just received from the doctor. Gray was taken a-back. It was though he was all set up to give Ruben and me an ass chewing, and I broke his rhythm. Ruben's face dropped with concern, and he ignored Gray's weak attempts to continue asking questions. Ruben started asking me questions about my doctor's visit. Gray was agitated that he had lost control of this little meeting. He asked me a question, and Ruben answered it for me. Gray fired back at Ruben, "Let her answer her own questions. What are you, her attorney!" Ruben's face got red, and his cheek twitched. I braced myself to be able to jump in between them. I looked at Ruben, and with my facial expressions he knew what I was thinking: let it go, calm down. He took a deep breath, looked at me and said, "Are you all right?" I felt my eyes welling up with water, so I turned my head. I didn't want Gray to see weakness. Gray took mercy on me and said, "Hey, I hope things come out okay on Thursday. Now get out of here." I got up and went to the restroom.

When I came back down the hall past Gray's office, I could hear him beyond his closed door, talking to Ruben like a dog. I stopped just short of his office, and tried to eavesdrop. Evantie came down the hall toward me, so I continued walking towards the back computer room. Later as I approached my office, I could hear Ruben and Gray were now in Ruben's and my office. I heard Ruben say with controlled rage, "David, I'm going to ask you for the last time to stop talking to me like this. I'm not yelling at you." As I entered the office, Gray grabbed me by the shoulders, and asked me to step back outside. Ruben said, "No way Gray, I want her to witness this." Gray pushed me outside and shut the door. I heard Ruben tell Gray, "I'm not putting up with this Gray," and Ruben walked out of the office. Gray started to follow Ruben down the hall towards the door, and then he saw me walking towards Ruben. Gray stopped and ducked into his office.

I walked Ruben out, and asked him if he was okay. Ruben said, "Did you hear any of that?" I answered, "I heard enough. Ruben, he's just pushing your buttons and trying to get you to blow up. David Gray's doing Lawrence Evantie's dirty work for him." Ruben responded, "I know, and I didn't buy into it at all. Weren't you proud of me?" I said, "Yes, very. You did a good job of controlling yourself, and he's the one that lost it. He sounded like a maniac." Ruben got into his car, and reached out his hand to shake mine. He said, "Hey Dar, don't worry too much about this MRI stuff. There's no way you have M.S. You're in too good of shape. It's just probably something stupid, like AIDs or something." We both smiled and laughed, and I called him a rat-bastered.

As I walked back down the hall towards my desk, Mattivi pulled me into his office. He told me that Evantie was looking for me, that the acting Commissioner of Customs was about to call, and that the Commissioner wanted me to brief him. I sat down, closed my eyes, and shook my head, thinking, this is just all I need. Concerned, Mattivi asked, "Hey, are you all right? You don't look your gorgeous self, What's wrong?" Just then Evantie summoned me so I went into his office. He handed me the phone, and I briefed the Acting Commissioner, Stan Wallace. Wallace sounded nice enough for a politician, and thanked me for the great job that I was doing. I felt like if I were a baby, he'd be kissing me on the cheek. I hate politicians! They are as shallow as teaspoons.

Chapter 11

The Botched Controlled Delivery

The tanker car had been delivered to San Bernardino, was under surveillance, and my warrant was written. Three days after the tanker car was delivered to San Bernardino, I got a call from Ruben. Just the day prior, Evantie had very stupidly pulled surveillance from the tanker car, assuming that we had given it enough time. I argued this decision to no avail. It had been my experience to see crooks wait weeks before attempting to pick up a large load. This gives the crooks a chance to counter-surveillance the load, and see if it's cool or not. Crooks also know how stingy cops will be about footing the bill for a manpower intensive surveillance.

I was at the U.S. Attorney's office with Yvette when I got Ruben's call. When he started off this phone call with, "Are you sitting down?" I knew something was wrong. Ruben explained how the day after Evantie pulled surveillance off of the controlled delivery (tanker car), the crooks popped the top and made entry. I responded, "What! How the hell did they do that. That's impossible!" Ruben said, "No, it's not Dar, it's the damndest thing. They "Jerry-Rigged" a mechanism with a tri-pod and a pulley, and extracted the hatch-port valve system with two forklifts. (The valve system is a system of valves that extend from the opening of the hatch on top of the tanker car to the bottom of the car, used to fill and extract the commodity as well as pressurize or depressurize). When they hoisted up the valve system, and saw that their load was gone, they split. They even left some of their tools there." I couldn't believe what I was hearing. I was so pissed off. I briefed Yvette, and she and I were both extremely frustrated with the situation. I told her, "If only Evantie had left surveillance crew on for just one more day, we would have gotten the off-load crew." Yvette said, "I can't believe that they wouldn't keep surveillance on this for just a couple of more days. I've had agencies watch controlled deliveries for weeks." I was embarrassed that my agency had done this, and was convinced that their lack of support for my case was because of the grievances filed by Ruben and I. Had Easel the weasel been the case agent on this case, surveillance on the tanker car would have lasted two or three weeks, and Ruben and I both knew it. I could also sense that Yvette was beginning to see a pattern of non-support for me from my agency. I knew that she was beginning to see that something was very wrong here. As embarrassed as I was, I was also glad that someone else, especially a federal prosecutor, was seeing with their own two eyes what my agency was capable of. Yvette was both very smart, and objective. It was important that she began to see what was going on here. I wouldn't know until later, just how important.

Ruben, Renado, and I spent the rest of the week running down leads, fighting with the FBI, and meeting with Yvette.

Darlene with Task Force Officers during controlled delivery cross country

Chapter 12

Internal Affairs

On the evening of April 14, 1998, I got a call at home from Lawrence Evantie. He stated that, "Some lady from San Francisco will be coming to the office tomorrow to talk to you about your EEO case." I reminded him that I had approved sick leave for a doctor's appointment on Thursday afternoon. He said that I could come in the morning, and still make it in plenty of time for my testing. I said, "O.K." I thought that this might be a good thing as maybe someone was finally going to take this EEO stuff seriously, and investigate it. I couldn't sleep that night. I was too worried about what this MRI might bring. Ben tried to comfort me but I could see the worry on his face.

The next morning, April 15, 1998, I went to the office. It wasn't long before Evantie intercommed me to his office. He introduced me to Lana Janston, Group Supervisor from San Francisco. Evantie left the office and closed the door on us. As he was leaving, Evantie had this evil smirk on his face, and I knew there was something up. Ms. Janston informed me that I was under investigation for wrongful release of information. She began reading me my rights, and I interrupted her, and told her that Evantie had told me last night that she was there to talk to me about my EEO complaint. Janston replied that the investigation did involve my EEO complaint. I then told her that I wasn't going to talk to her until I spoke to my attorney. She ordered me to sign the rights warning and I told her that I had approved sick leave today and walked out of the office. I went to my desk, and 911 paged my attorney. Ruben was sitting there and asked what was going on. As I briefed him, the phone rang. It was my attorney, whom I briefed. He then asked to speak to Ms. Janston, and I obliged.

Ruben was pissed. He said, "What a chicken-shit thing to do, knowing about your medical test today and all. Hang in there Dar, don't let them get to you." I could feel my blood boiling. After a few minutes, Ms. Janston came over the intercom telling me to pick up line 3, it was my attorney. He said, "It's a witch hunt; they are saying that you wrongfully released information that was contained in your EEO report. Look, they are violating your Title 7 rights and Privacy Act rights, but you have to participate in this grilling, or they can fire you. Now, go to your doctors appointment, and afterwards you and I will talk more about strategy before you go in there. O.K.?" I answered, "All right," and left for my appointment. My husband Ben surprised me by showing up at the clinic. I was so glad to see him. I briefed him on the bullshit investigation. Ben said, "That Evantie, he's a real piece of work huh." Ben stayed with me during my entire test, comforted me, and went back to work. They told me it would be a week or so before I got the results back on my test.

I talked strategy with my attorney and went back to the office where I signed the rights warning and answered Ms. Janston's stupid questions. She told me that this was all about the letters of commendation that I had included in my EEO complaint. These letters of commendation were from prosecutors and DEA supervisors commending me on all of my work. I didn't even write these letters, they did. In the course of these letters they put in several case numbers, and names of bad guys. I included these letters in my complaint to demonstrate that I was an outstanding agent. Just then it hit me, there were very similar hero letters hanging up and down the walls of this office. I showed Janston the photos, and reminded her that the office has a cleaning team as well as other non-agency personnel who routinely enter the office and view these photos. She just smirked at me.

The questions that Ms. Janston had were all designed to elicited a yes or no answer. If I had followed her instructions to simply answer them with a mere yes or no with no explanation on my part, the statement would have appeared very damning to me. So I refused to answer with only yes or no and insisted on writing out an explanation to this witch-hunt. She reminded me several times that she had a plane to catch, and that she didn't intend for this interview to last this long. I said, "Fuck you," under my breath and took my time, doing the best job that I could under these stressful circumstances. It took me five hours to complete my statement. Ms. Janston missed her plane.

The timing of this investigation was brilliant on their part. The promotion list for GS 13 had just been released, and I was in the top 10. There were 11 openings, and I was assured to get a promotion. The only way that they could promote someone over me was if I had a red file (an active open Internal Affairs investigation). By policy, no one can be promoted with a red file. They couldn't find anything legitimate to go after me, so they just made shit up. They knew it wouldn't stick, but that wasn't the purpose. They had accomplished their mission, and I was taken off the list. That night, I went to the gym before I went home. I swam until I could barely pull myself out of the pool. All I could see was Evantie's arrogant smirk as he called me into his office and Janston began reading me my rights. I started having the dream again, but something woke me up, and I couldn't get back to sleep.

The next day Ruben, Jerry, Renado, Mattivi, Gray, and I hit a business in San Bernardino as well as several other houses connected to the tanker car seizure. Two days later, after endless interviews and running down leads, I arrested a key player in the infamous Arellano-Felix Narcotics Organization. I flipped him (term used for getting defendants to cooperate), and Yvette and I put him in protective custody, and began interviewing the CI (confidential informant). Yvette and I had lunch together, and she asked me why I wasn't getting any help on my case. I had authored, presented, and achieved OCDETF (Organized Crime

Drug Enforcement Task Force) status for this case, and for the Rail project. This meant that I was supposed to be supplied with a full task force to handle this investigation and project. Evantie and SAIC Brinkley had pulled all of my support. I laughed sarcastically when I told her, "You're looking at the OCDETF task force of me, myself, and I." I trusted Yvette, and told her what was going on. She looked at me and said, "They can't do that, that's undermining a criminal case in order to shut you up." I shook my head. Yvette replied in a very disturbed voice, "You know, there's a word for this…Obstruction of Justice."

The day after my working lunch with Yvette, April 19, 1998, I had my doctor's appointment. I was very relieved to hear that I didn't have M.S. The doctor did, however, tell me that Epstein Bar Syndrome, commonly referred to as Mono, caused the ringing in my ears and several other symptoms. He said I had probably gotten it from the pool I had been swimming in. He added that because I had the virus for so long, undiagnosed, with an extended low-grade fever, the ringing in my ears would probably be permanent. My blood pressure was also extremely low, and my white blood cell count was very high. He told me that my body fat content was so low that it was messing up my menstrual cycle and causing a hormonal imbalance. Extended exhaustion, continued lack of deep "REM" sleep, and too much stress were taking their toll. But other than that, I was just fine. He looked at me and asked what was going on in my life that was causing all of this. I just starred back at him, smirked sarcastically, looked down at the ground, shook my head and laughed. He said, "I'm glad you find this all amusing; but you won't find it so funny when you're in the morgue, Agent Catalan." He gave me several prescriptions and told me that I had better slow down and get some rest.

That night the dream came, and I was back at Fort Huachuca Arizona, my last assignment as a Captain on active duty with the Military Police Corps. I was in my old office sitting in my chair. I remembered how that building smelled of old wood. It felt comfortable to be back there, like seeing an old friend again. I loved the Army, and always felt in control there. Things were simpler then. The little toddler appeared in the hallway in front of me. He was filthy and crying and began walking away. He looked back at me and motioned with his beautiful deep blue, mesmerizing eyes for me to follow him down the dark stairs. We walked into what used to be the old morgue area. He turned to me and smiled, causing a strange sensation of calm and peacefulness to come over me. As I began slowly walking towards him, I noticed that I had my dress blues on. I took his delicate, little, dirty hand in my white glove and then was startled awake by my alarm. I ran into the bathroom and barfed.

Chapter 13

Routine Business

On April 22, 1998, our office had to serve a search warrant in East L.A. We met in Costello Park in the parking lot by the pool. As I sat there waiting for the other agents to show up, I thought about why the name of this place was Costello Park. Lou Costello, of the famous "Abbott and Costello" had built the park in honor of his son. Costello's son had evidentially drowned, and Lou Costello wanted kids to have the opportunity to learn how to swim so that another drowning might be prevented. I thought of how painful it must of been to have lost a child and almost started crying. I know that I would just die if I lost one of my kids, and I worried so about the reoccurring dream I was having. I was afraid that it was some sort of warning. A part of me wished that I could quit my job and stay home with my kids so that I always knew that they were all right.

I worked on my EEO retaliation filing on my laptop, while I waited for the guys. We briefed in the parking lot, suited up and waited for the tow truck. The house that we were going to hit had a cast iron security gate on the door and iron bars on the windows. The plan was to hook the tow truck's hook and wench onto the front door, and have the tow truck pull the door off, after we gave "knock notice"(legal requirement to announce warrant entry before actual entry is made). When we arrived at the house, I grabbed the hook and ran toward the door. As I approached the porch, I knew that this was a bad idea. The house was old, and had one of those old porches with brick pillars holding up the porch roof. I hooked the door, and ran off of the porch. Jerry Johnston and a uniformed LAPD officer yelled, "Federal Agents with a search warrant, open the door." Just then the tow truck floored it, and the door went flying through the air, and crashed into the brick pillars. Just as the brick pillar collapsed, and the porch roof started to cave in, I noticed that there was an old black man standing there in the doorway, with his hand where the door knob use to be. This poor man had a complete look of shock on his face.

This was probably one of the most hilarious things I had ever seen. As we were running up to the house to make entry, everyone was laughing so hard we could barely make it through the door. As we secured the house, and completed the search, we all walked outside to look at the porch. We stood there cracking up laughing. If I hadn't seen it with my own two eyes, I'd never believed it. Just then, I noticed the old black man with two officers, sitting in a chair on his front yard. He was crying, and looking up at the damage to his home. His son was the one that the warrant was directed towards, yet he was the one who received the damage. All the sudden I stopped laughing, and it wasn't funny anymore. I felt a tremendous amount of guilt and sorrow for what we had done to this poor old man. I thought about my aging father, and how he'd feel if the home that he had worked so hard for many years had been damaged by a bunch of arrogant federal agents. I felt my stomach start to burn.

I went back to the office and attempted to finish my EEO complaint. I found it very hard to concentrate as I just kept thinking of that poor old man. I was angry at myself that I didn't try to somehow console him, and felt guilty that I had laughed so about the visual comedy of the situation. I finished the complaint and faxed it to the EEO office. This was a complaint of retaliation, based upon the foolish IA investigation regarding letters of commendation I had submitted in my original EEO complaint. This complaint was subsequently dismissed by the Regional Complaint Center on June 26, 1998, with no informal or formal investigation (i.e. none of my witnesses nor I were ever contacted by an EEO counselor on these specific issues). I filed a response to this dismissal on July 1,1998, stating the lack of investigation on these issues. To no one's surprise, I never received any response to either my complaint or my letter.

May 22, 1998, I read the article in the San Diego Union-Tribune dated May 16, 1998, regarding the lawsuit between Ricardo Sandoval and the U.S. Customs Service. Ervin Rios sent Ruben and I a copy. Rios is "Good People." Ricardo Sandoval recently won a lawsuit against Customs winning $200,000.00 and $500,000.00 in attorney's fees and back pay for discrimination. Sandoval used the same attorneys that Ruben, Sandy, Ervin Rios, and I initially used. On the last page of the article I took particular notice to the fact that Sandoval has filed a second lawsuit charging that after he alleged existence of a racist ring, he was subjected to a series of internal investigations and accused of crimes.

When I read this I had very mixed emotions. I felt consoled that someone who has experienced treatment similar to what I am receiving from my agency, won against Customs. I also became very worried. If they would come after someone like him (already a GS13 and a SA for the office of Internal Affairs) then I'm doomed. I feared that it would be only a matter of time before the other shoe drops right on my head. I also feared that because this agency lost so badly on the Sandoval Case, Customs will be out for blood, and it could easily be mine.

I called Sandy and read her the article. I told her that I found it very "apropos" for Customs to use a lawyer from the U.S. Attorney's office, and not from our own regional council. To me that is a big indication as to the confidence, or lack there of, our agency has in its own Regional Council. I remember thinking, who knows, maybe Sandy's right. Maybe Customs will be more leery about coming after us now that they have lost the Sandoval lawsuit. You would think that this agency would learn its lesson, but I feared not. There was a quote in this article from one of the jurors in this case that I found most haunting. Juror Cannon stated that, "Discrimination inside the government is no worse or more widespread that in corporate America," but he added, "The government has a lot more power, and that's when it becomes dangerous." If the general public only knew the power and control that management in this agency possesses over its employees and how they flaunt it, the general public would be disgusted. If my agency feels that we are a threat, they most certainly will be sicking their IA dogs on us.

On June 25, 1998, I was investigated for the second time by my agency for wrongful use of Government Identification. Evidently, someone anonymously called into the IA (Internal Affairs) office and made a false accusation that I was using my reserve Army identification to gain access to military flights at a reduced or free rate. I was required to commute three hours, one way, from my home, to the IA office in Long Beach, CA., for this Witch-Hunt, Part 2. When I got there, IA Agent, Terry Clay escorted me into an interview room. As I sat there getting my rights read to me again, I realized just what it was like to be facing a large glass mirror, that I knew others were watching from the other side; the same position that I had put witnesses, and defenders in too many times to count. The world looks a lot different when you're sitting on the other side of that table, and someone is firing the questions at you. I felt my stomach burn and my anger rise up to my face. My body felt hot with rage all over.

I explained to the IA rocket scientist in a low, controlled rage tone of voice that "The use of ones military I.D. for this purpose is common practice within the Army, it's commonly referred to as "catching a hop" or "space available." It is not a violation of any policy, and I never did this." Additionally, if it were a violation of policy, that policy would be under the jurisdiction of U.S. Army Criminal Investigation Division (CID), not U.S. Customs service. So basically Terry, all of this was done without you having the sense enough to even check if my alleged offense was even a violation." I grabbed the written version of the rights they read me and made me sign, pointed at it, and said, "I want a copy of this. This bullshit is over." At first Terry refused to give me a copy, but after several verbal altercations and non-verbal indicators of threat from me, I left with a copy. This would be the only evidence I had that I had ever been there for this amazing blunder.

That evening I went to the gym and ran five miles. With every step I took, I felt as though I was going to explode. My chest was tight and felt like I had an elephant standing on it. I knew that, once again, this IA Witch Hunt occurred when I had made the BQL for promotion to GS 13, giving me a red file and eliminating me from the BQL. This was a cheap, but clever, shot designed to put pressure on me not to testify on Ruben's upcoming deposition for his federal law suit against Customs and to teach me a lesson. I felt like a little helpless kid being bullied by the neighborhood thug.

That night I had the dream again. I was standing in my bedroom and the beautiful blond haired, blue-eyed toddler appeared before me. He was filthy and had tears in his eyes. I picked him up and took him to the sink in my bedroom and sat him down. I took a washcloth and began to try to clean his little hands. He looked at me with his angelic eyes, took my hand and smiled. The next thing I knew was that I was standing in a beautiful pasture holding him. The grass was Technicolor green and waved in the wind as it blew. There were cattle grazing everywhere. I put the toddler down, he took my hand, and motioned for me to come with him.

We walked up to the top of a small hill overlooking a pleasant valley. There was a beautiful older looking farmhouse that someone was adding construction to. Not too far from the house was a corral. There were cattle chutes where one steers cattle into in order to inoculate them. Between the flat fence posts, I could see the back of a young man, working the cows toward one of the chutes. I attempted to move closer, but for some reason I couldn't. As much as I could tell, the man seemed to be in his early to mid 30's. He was just under 6 ft and a little stocky, not fat. He had short brown hair, and was wearing a flannelled, checked shirt, blue jeans and boots. I could begin to hear his deep raspy voice as he coaxed the cows. He spoke with either a British or Australian accent. I then noticed that he had two dogs working with him. One of the dogs was biting at the heels of the cows. The man yelled at the dog, calling it mate. Although he sounded a lot like Mel Gibson, the actor, somehow I knew it wasn't him. This man was very angelic and spiritual.

I began to notice something very strange. I could see off at a distance what appeared to be a kangaroo bouncing around. I could also see a pond close by with ducks. Everything was so beautiful and peaceful. The man's voice, though deep and at times gritty, seemed very comforting and almost familiar to me, yet somehow I knew that this was a stranger. I noticed that he had an old flatbed truck sitting close, with two packs of cigarettes lying on the hood. One was wadded up, and the other had just been opened. There were beautiful colorful, wildflowers dotting parts of the grass. I wanted so badly to stay there and walk over to see whom this stranger was. Then I felt the toddler squeezing my hand, and I knew it was time to go. I took one last look and attempted to see the face of the man. I kept hoping that he would turn our way and see us there, but he didn't.

The next morning when I awoke, I lay there wondering what the hell all of this meant. Those few moments in that dream were the most peaceful ones that I had felt in years. I began wondering where this place could have been. I remembered the kangaroo and the accent of the man and wondered if it was Australia, but that couldn't be right. From what I knew about Australia, it was pretty dry, brown, and rocky, kind of like west Texas. Why did the toddler take me there, and why wasn't I allowed to see the face of the man? Do these dreams have any meaning, or am I just cracking under pressure? And the location. Why in the hell was I in either Australia or England? Why not my beautiful home in the Appalachian Mountains of Kentucky. None of this made any sense. I thought of something I heard a LAPD narcotics officer say to me. He said that in LAPD they were only allowed to work

major narcotics for three years for fear of burn out. I had been working major narcotics investigations for 11 years. I was convinced that I
was losing my mind. I wanted so badly to tell Ben, Ruben or maybe
even Sandy about these dreams, but I had this sense that I was supposed to keep this a secret, like I would be breaking some sort of confidence or something. I was also afraid that they would lock me in a
rubber room.

The next day, I filed an EEO complaint of retaliation regarding the
Witch-Hunt, Number 2. EEO Supervisor Conales never assigned me an
investigator for this issue. I know she received the complaint, because I
faxed it and certified mailed it. I had both the fax transmittal and the
certified mail to prove she got the complaint. I followed this up with
leaving her a voice mail on her phone. What a blatant arrogant witch
this woman was.

On June 25, 1998, SA Edwin Easel (Easel the weasel), the office
moron and resident kiss ass, was promoted to GS 13, having a lower
CAAPS score than mine. Had Winkowsky followed policy, he would
have reported Easel for the taking heroin home incident, and Easel
would have received the mandatory 90 days on the bricks, or even firing, eliminating him from this promotion. When Ruben and I confirmed this news, we both became ill. We left the office early that day in
preparation for the "dumpster diving" I had to do that night. We knew
that this would give us an opportunity to talk.

I went home and tried to get some sleep. All I did was toss and turn.
I was full of rage that they had promoted Easel the weasel over Ruben
and I. This guy had much less time in Customs than we did, not to
mention no prior law enforcement experience, and the inability to
make a case on his own without being spoon-fed. My stomach
burned, so I gave up and went to the frig to get some milk. The phone
rang and it was Sandy. She said, "I heard the news. What a crock of
shit. You and Ruben run circles around that weasel, and everyone
knows it. If this isn't blatant retaliation I don't know what is." She

spent most of the conversation trying to console me. Sandy's the best girlfriend I ever had. She was the most honest person I'd ever met, not to mention, the most loyal friend. I needed this phone call; it lifted my spirits.

That night I got ready for my trash run. This was for a fraud case that I had on this businessman in Temecula, CA. This crook had completed a "Corporate Bleed-Out" of his business, and had put the screws to all the other partners, and employees. He had also filed a phony bankruptcy. He had made a lot of money via the business that he was bankrupting, thus having the need to launder this money through other front companies overseas. When he wired the money back and forth, he committed several Customs violations, including money laundering. I was going that night to his business to dig in his trash dumpster (hence the slang dumpster diving), for documents, or other evidence. You'd be surprised at what stupid crooks throw away in their trash.

When I got there at about midnight, Ruben and Jerry Johnston were already there. I was on time, but they still gave me shit about making them wait. Like me, neither one of them could take a nap. We were all tired and grouchy. They set up their surveillance on me in the adjacent parking lot. I snuck over to the dumpsters. As I approached the back of the crook's business, I could smell something horrible. It smelled like a skunk. I looked around and couldn't see anything, so I jumped into the dumpster. Just then I heard and felt a loud thug at the bottom of the dumpster. Out ran a very large skunk. I ducked down in the dumpster, held my breath, and squinted my eyes shut. I then heard laughter, off at a distance. Ruben and Jerry were cracking up laughing. I began laughing with them. Although I got lucky and the skunk didn't spray me directly, I still smelled of trash and skunk.

I found some great documents and other evidence, and returned to the parking lot where Jerry and Ruben were still laughing at me. I had parked my car a distance away, and needed a lift to my car. Jerry said, "Hop in the back of my truck here woman, you sure as hell aren't riding in my cab." I looked at Rube and he was cracking up laughing at me, and said, "Don't look at me, you stink, you're not riding in my car." I said, "Never mind assholes, I'll walk." They followed me to my car making stinky jokes the whole way, and having a great time at my expense. I didn't care; I was happy that I had gotten just what I needed to nail the crook for fraud and money laundering. It had all been worth it. The next day, I briefed my fraud AUSA (Assistant United States Attorney) on this case, Jim McNarra, and he was very pleased.

Chapter 14

Disciplinary Action

On July 30, 1998, EEO Supervisor Conales lied in a statement regarding the reason for the removal of my EEO counselor Anna Francisco. She stated that she had spoken with Francisco on numerous occasions about following the time requirements, insinuating that Anna was somehow being deficient in her duties. Conales stated of her intention to remove her as early as October 1997. I called up Anna and read the statement to her. She was appalled. Anna told me that Conales never mentioned any of this to her. Anna just confirmed what I already knew. Conales was a snake extraordinaire.

On August 3, 1998, I was in my office typing up reports on the computer when Evantie came in and said, "Hey Dar, can you come see me please?" I thought, oh great; what the hell's this all about. Ruben wasn't there, and I was hesitant to walk into Evantie's office with no witness, but I did anyway. I went into his office and Evantie said, "Why don't you shut the door." I responded in a very respectful and professional tone of voice, "I'd rather not sir." Evantie smirked and shook his head condescendingly, and said "O.K." He handed me a letter of disciplinary action for wrongful release of information, based upon the letters of commendation I had given to Anna in my EEO complaint. This was now just a few weeks before I was scheduled to testify in Ruben's federal lawsuit.

I glossed over the letter, and knew I had to somehow control my temper. I very sarcastically said to Evantie, "Is that it?" He responded, "Well don't you have any questions or anything?" I answered no, and turned to walk away. Evantie stopped me and said, "Well you have to sign here where you received the letter." I walked to his desk, grabbed the pen from his fancy pen holder, signed the document, and attempted to leave. He said, "Hay Dar, wait a minute. How's that fraud case coming along?" I briefed him of how positive the prosecutor was, and the fact that we were confident that based upon what was seized in prior warrants and in my trash runs, we would most certainly be able to get this guy on fraud and money laundering charges. Evantie immediately began to ask questions, in a very negative way. It was clear that he was trying to undermine my case. I got frustrated with his subversive line of questioning, and told him, "Hay, if you don't like what were doing on the case, go talk to the prosecutor yourself." He responded with, "Well I just may do that. You've been on this thing way too long, and I obviously need to move this guy along, and get this thing wrapped up." I said, "You do that Evantie, you do that."

I went back to my desk and read the letter. I took particular note that on the last page of this letter, there was a paragraph that was coercive as hell. The paragraph read, "A copy of this letter will be placed in your Official Personnel Folder (OPF) for a period not to exceed three (3) years from the date of the letter. The letter may be removed by local management, with my concurrence, should circumstances warrant such action." I thought to myself, gee, I wonder what these circumstances would be—Ah, drop your EEO complaint and refuse to testify for Ruben. If I did this, I'm sure that all will be well. It was signed by Dirk Kirkland of the disciplinary review board. Everyone in Customs knows that Kirkland is one of Brinkley's crony's. Now this asshole has empowered local management, the very same people who we have filed these complaints about, to be in a position to magically make this letter disappear if I play ball.

Ruben walked in and saw me about to blow up. He asked, "What's going on Dar? What's the matter?" I tossed the letter over to him. He began reading it, stopped, came over to my desk, grabbed me, and hustled me and the letter out to his car. We went for a ride, and I read him the whole letter, and told him of how Evantie was now planning to undermine my fraud case. I told Ruben of how the average fraud case, unlike dope cases, usually takes about three years to develop, and I had only worked on this one for a little over a year. Ruben told me not to worry, that it was just another scare tactic trying to get me to blow up. He reminded me of how ludicrous this was, and of how it's just because they can't find anything else on me so they had to come up with something. That night I went to the gym again and swam until I almost drowned. I lost count of laps and of time. I was sore the next day.

On August 5th, 1998, Evantie and I met with my federal prosecutor McNarra on my fraud case. I had previously met numerous times with this prosecutor, and he was extremely pleased with my work and progress on this case. It would be interesting to see just how Evantie was going to try to torpedo this case with a very positive prosecutor. The prosecutor briefed Evantie on our progress and our intensions with the case. I wouldn't have believed it if I hadn't seen it and heard it with my own two eyes and ears. Evantie actually had the balls to try to undermine me with the prosecutor. He kept making comments that were clearly meant to make me look bad, and my prosecutor, much to Evantie's dismay, was defending me. As the meeting went on, AUSA McNarra was looking at me with suspicious facial expressions as if to say, "What the hell's going on here."

When the meeting was over, Evantie left and I stayed behind to brief McNarra. As soon as I shut his door for privacy he said, "What the hell's going on here Dar?" I responded, "This is what happens in our agency when you are not part of the "Good Old boy" system." McNarra looked at me with pity, and shook his head. I was embarrassed and really didn't want to get into all this petty crap with him, so I didn't. I just assured him not to worry about Evantie, that I'd take care of everything, and that things would be cool. I was just happy that Evantie wasn't successful in his transparent efforts to torpedo me with my prosecutor. I was happy that this AUSA saw right through his tactics, and didn't fall for them. I reminded myself that against a federal prosecutor, Evantie was about as bright as a burnt out light bulb.

That night I was so hoping that my toddler would come and get me and take me back to that farm. I tossed and turned all night. My stomach was burning, and I couldn't sleep. The toddler didn't come for me.

On August 7, 1998, at approximately 1400hrs, I checked my Customs in-box. I found photocopies of reports of investigation (ROI's) of closed cases. There were notes on these ROI's from our new acting Group Supervisor Dudley O'Shea, asking me to modify or explain them. Dudley O'Shea was another of Brinkley's well-known crony's. O'Shea's wife was the SAIC (Special Agent In Charge)/Los Angeles, Internal Affairs Office. Other supervisors who had previously approved these ROI's displayed no concerns about them when approved. I have never in my almost 11 years of service in the agency observed agents being made to modify reports on closed cases; and even if I wanted to modify them, our computer system won't allow you to modify ROI's once approved.

Additionally, I canvassed the RAIC/Riverside office, and no other agents were being required to complete this type of task on closed cases. I asked Bob Mattivi, old salt, with almost 30 years of experience and smartest guy in the office, if he had ever observed anything like this. Bob shook his head is disbelief, and said, "Boy Darlene, O'Shea's only been on the job a couple of days, and he's already going after you." Bob had never seen anything like this. Bob Mattivi had forgotten more about criminal investigations than guys like O'Shea ever knew. I trusted Bob and knew that he was right on the money.

On August 11, 1998, I observed SSA Terry Clay, "Mr. IA," walking down the hall of our office. I took particular note to the fact that he was walking right past all of the hero photos hanging on the walls that had a hell of a lot more information in them then the ones I got investigated/disciplined for. As I passed him, I looked at one of the photos, causing him to also look. I looked back at him with a pompous smirk and shook my head. He got my point, looked embarrassed, and kept walking. As I walked to my office I realized that the new GS 13 list had just come out, and I had once again made the BQL (best qualified list). I felt worn down and futile. I knew that I was about to be investigated again on some bullshit charge, again tagging me with a red file and tossing me off the list. I went home in disgust.

On August 17, 1998, I filed a response to my letter of disciplinary action. Shortly thereafter, I received a response from Kirkland (Brinkley's crony friend, hand picked by Brinkley for this position). His response stated the following, "You expressed very strong concerns in your grievance letter that the letter of reprimand contained language you found coercive in nature. Please be advised that the language in the reprimand which states (if you should separate from the Service before this letter is removed from your OPF, it will be removed and destroyed in accordance with applicable regulation)." I thought to myself, how clever for Mr. Kirkland to change the actual wording of this letter and conveniently leave out the part about "if circumstances warrant local management may remove this letter." I read the letter to Ruben and said, "What a moron!"

I called Sandy that night, as I do most every night. My husband thinks that we chatter about this stuff too much, and get each other in an uproar. I don't know, maybe he's right. Still, Sandy and I do a good job of motivating each other to fight back. Sandy is one brave little chick, and I have a lot of respect for her opinion; not to mention that I sometimes need to hear a woman's view on things. I'm in a male dominated field, surrounded by men all day, and all that testosterone can start to have an effect on a person. Sandy cheered me up, as she always does, and I was grateful for it. Sandy truly has a heart of gold.

September 3, 1998, I went to the U.S. Attorney's office for a meeting with Yvette. Aftewards I spoke with Arnold Connez. He informed me that in the last two staff meetings, SAIC Brinkley got up in front of all of the supervisor and trashed the people who were filing EEO complaints and the EEO process. He also stated that Brinkley had mentioned Sandy and me by name and stated that we were troublemakers and that I was a hot head. That night when I got home, Sandy, Shannon Getz, and I had a phone conversation. Shannon stated that another supervisor, Ron James, had told her the same thing. Ron James was my first supervisor in Customs and also one of the nicest men I have ever met; however, he was also lacking in the balls department, and I knew I couldn't count on him to testify as to what he had heard. I reminded myself that not all managers in Customs were evil; there were those who were evil with balls, there were those who were evil with no balls and there were those who were not evil, and had no balls. We decided to file a Class Action EEO Complaint, and when we later pitched this idea to Ruben, Ervin Rios, Ricardo Sandoval and Arnold Connez, they agreed. I was elected to write up the complaint. I stayed up until midnight that night writing the damn thing. My husband said that my incredible writing abilities could sometimes be a double-edged sword. I agreed. Sandy did her usual excellent editing job and we submitted it.

Chapter 15

Threat via Mail

September 9th, 1998, I woke up this morning hoping that this stuff was all just some sort of bizarre dream. When I got home from work that day I checked the mail. It's funny, when I got it from the box it looked like an invitation of some type for my kids. I took it into the house along with the other mail, and began sorting through everything. I opened the bills first, may as well get the bad news out of the way, and then threw away the junk mail. My kids were all trying to talk to me at once, the way kids always do when you first come home from work. They all want your complete attention, and thus I was only half paying attention to what was there—junk mail, bill, Ben and me.

With all of my training and experience in terrorism and letter bombs, you would think that I would have noticed that this letter didn't have a return address on the outside. As I was listening to all my kids talk to me at once, I opened the innocent looking "invitation." At first I only noticed that it was ripped, and folded like a child folds notes and places them inside these types of small envelopes. I thought it was just a note or invitation for one of my kids. As I responded to my kids as they told me about their days, I smoothed out the wrinkles of the letter and wondered why it was ripped. Then I read the words, "SHUT UP AND RESIGN OR YOUR FLETC PICTURES WILL BE MAILED TO THE TABLOIDS AND YOUR FAMILY WILL BE HUMILIATED."

A familiar feeling came over me. My body felt weak, and I recognized this feeling from an incident that happened when I was younger. I was about eight years old when I saw my neighbor shoot another neighbor right in front of me. I couldn't believe what I was seeing. I watched my neighbor Vernon Steller being threatened by this huge guy we all called "Crazy Dave," and could see the fear and anger on Mr. Steller's face. I knew something awful was about to happen. As Mr. Steller watched Crazy Dave Jackson storm away to his house, the anguish and fear grew on the smaller man's face. Mr. Steller then ran into his own home. His little boy, Ryan, was running behind him pulling on his clothes begging him, "Don't dad don't, please don't," as if he already knew what was about to happen. I watched this with most curiosity, wondering what this little boy knew that I didn't.

Then Mr. Steller came out of the house with his son Ryan hanging on his arm, still begging him to stop. Mr. Steller had a gun, and I felt numb. I had been riding my bike, and had stopped to observe this argument, and now I was frozen there not able to move. My mind was racing in fear for little Ryan. I wanted to grab him away from this and run with him to my house, but I couldn't move. Mr. Steller began yelling, "Come on outside, now's the time, now's the time," Finally someone appeared at the door of the Witherspout's house, only it wasn't Crazy Dave. It was his brother-in-law Mr. Witherspout. Mr. Witherspout seemed not to be so mad and crazy, but I thought that he only wanted to come out and diffuse the situation. I felt a short-lived sense of relief. Mr. Witherspout always seemed to be a nice, calm, practical kind of guy, and I thought he'd be able to reason with Mr. Steller.

The two men met in front of this large tree that looked like a Christmas tree that stood between their two houses. How queer it seemed that this took place in front of the very tree that these two neighbors argued so much about. I never understood why Mr. Steller hated that tree so much. I always thought it was a beautiful tree, particularly in the winter when decorated for Christmas. I know now that their hatred had nothing to do with this beautiful tree.

The men were talking, and little Ryan was still begging his dad to go back into the house. Because they were talking and not shouting, I thought that everything would be all right. Then I heard a pop, and Mr. Waterspout fell to the ground moaning. Poor little Ryan started screaming and crying and pulling his dad back into his house. I looked into Mr. Steller's eyes. They looked dead and numb, just like I was feeling. Suddenly a rush of energy came to me and I flew on my bike and ran up the steps into my home. Everything around me didn't make sense, and as I tried to tell my parents what had just happened, I couldn't get my words to make sense either. It was just like I was dreaming all of this. Nothing seemed real to me. The air had a real queer smell, reminding me of the time I got shocked plugging in something and could smell the electricity running through my body.

I had long since forgotten that feeling. When I read this letter, I was there again. Nothing made sense around me, and the air smelt of electricity. I stood there frozen as my kids were talking to me. I wasn't hearing them. Suddenly my daughter, Rochelle, grabbed the letter and said, "Is this for me?" I grabbed the letter back, and tried not to show a reaction to my kids, for fear of alarming them. "No, this is for me," I said.

I went up stairs and tried to dial the phone. It took me many times to correctly page my husband 911. My fingers kept hitting the wrong numbers, as though I had no control over them. Finally I heard my husband's voice mail and I felt a sense of relief as I paged him to our home. The FLETC pictures this note was referring to were the pictures that were taken by my ex-boyfriend 10 years ago. We went through the Federal Law Enforcement Training Center (FLETC) together in Glynco, Georgia. This is the Department of Treasury's training academy for most of its federal employees, including federal agents. While at FLETC, I did a very stupid thing; hindsight is 20/20. I allowed my ex-boyfriend, a Customs employee, to take very explicit, embarrassing, nude photos of me, a mistake I'll regret now for the rest of my life. When I broke off the relationship, my ex-boyfriend was so angry, that the day after, he went to work and showed my pictures and those of several other women, to several Customs pilots and Air Interdiction Officers (AIOs).

As he was displaying our pictures, my ex-boyfriend was making very derogatory remarks about us.

The pilots and AIOs all knew me, and several of them took offense that he was doing this. One of them contacted Customs Internal Affairs, and my ex-boyfriend was investigated. The IA investigator, Donna Jones interviewed me and told me what my ex-boyfriend had done. She also informed me that she had seized the pictures, and that they would be destroyed upon conclusion of the investigation. My ex-boyfriend was forced to resign, and now works for another agency.

As I continued staring at this note, I began looking inside the envelope as though if I just kept looking hard enough, an explanation of what was going on here might magically appear. Then the phone rang. It was my husband. I told him what I had, and he reacted very unsurprised. He comforted me, and assured me that it was just a bluff to scare me. My husband is the wisest man I know, and even though I realized he was probably right, I still was in disbelief of what was happening. The air still smelled like electricity, and my body felt weak. I suddenly remembered that I was putting fingerprints all over the letter, and probably destroying any evidence that we would need to catch whoever did this. Once again, in my disbelief of what was happening to me, all of my training and experience had gone right out the window. I put the letter in a clear plastic bag.

I then called Sandy and told her what had just happened. The anger in her voice was so strong that it overpowered the numbness that I was feeling. She paged our attorney, and we then had a three-way conversation. Our attorney's reaction was very similar to my husband's, one of, "This doesn't surprise me, this agency is capable of anything; we've seen this behavior before." My attorney then said something that snapped me right out of my shock. He said that my agency, in order to defend themselves, will accuse me of sending this letter myself, in order to boost my law suit. When he said this, I became infuriated! This seemed the most ridiculous concept imaginable. Like I would embarrass my kids and my family to boost a lawsuit that, as of right now, is a slam-dunk anyway. As stupid as this sounded, I knew he was right. I knew that is exactly the lame tactic my agency would attempt. I told him that it wouldn't work because I would just pass a polygraph. He responded that polygraph's aren't accepted in Federal Civil Court. My feelings turned to rage.

Sandy and I then contacted Ervin Rios. We now had three enraged people on the phone, but I was the only one who expressed any shock at the situation. Ervin and Sandy were also very supportive and tried to console me. One thing about situations such as these, it sure does weed out the fair weather friends. Sandy, Ervin, and Ruben Sandoval, are rare true blue friends who understand the meaning of loyalty. After my conversation with Sandy and Ervin, I called Ruben. He was in disbelief also. His reaction was more similar to mine, on of complete shock. Ruben asked me if he could talk to a U.S. Attorney whom he knew very well and trusted and elicit advice from her. I agreed.

That night I couldn't sleep. Again, I wanted so badly for the toddler to take me to the beautiful farm and see the strange young man there. My stomach burned so badly that I had to, for the first time that I can ever remember, take Tums with my usual glass of milk. The toddler didn't come.

September 10th, I had to get up, go to work, and act as though nothing had happened just in case someone in my office was watching me to see my reaction. I took a half-day off, in order to meet with Ruben and Sandy at the U.S. Attorney's office. We had previously agreed (arrangements made before I received the note) to meet at the U.S. Attorney's office to sign a class EEO complaint that all of us, (Sandy, Ruben, Connez, Shannon Getz, Ervin Rios, Ricardo Sandoval and myself) had agreed to file. Before I left the office, I got a call from Ervin. He told me that he was so mad that he talked to the editor of the L A Times. I couldn't believe that he had done this. I was very angry with him, and I scolded him. He humbly apologized and told me that he was so angry that he just had to do something. I told him that he should have talked to me first because I was taking this to the U.S. Postal Inspectors to pursue this criminally, and the media would most certainly get in the way. Ervin again apologized, in a tone of voice that made me feel like I had just kicked a puppy. Ervin meant well, and I felt bad about scolding him. He had been there for me so many times before, I know he was just trying to do something that would make us not feel so helpless. Ervin is one of the most honest, big-hearted guys anyone will ever meet.

I met with Ruben and Sandy at the AUSA's office. Ruben told me that he talked to AUSA Penny Salvador. Penny told Ruben that I should put the original in a safe place like a safety deposit box or a safe. She also agreed that I should contact the Postal Inspectors and not give the original to them unless they guaranteed that my agency would in no way be involved in the investigation. Ruben told me that he has a safe, and offered to keep the original for me and make copies. I agreed. I trusted Ruben with my life. We had been partners in the field for many years now and had backed each other up in many a tight situations. We never dreamed in a million years that we would have to depend on each other so deeply, in this type of situation.

I was running late for my meeting with our attorney, and my stress level was over the breaking point. I was on the I-10 freeway, when my pager went off. It was my husband's pager number with a 911 suffix. With everything that was happening, I immediately thought of the worst. I got off of the freeway in a bad part of LA and began to panic. I couldn't find a pay phone anywhere, and when I did, it was broken. Finally I found a pay phone, and called my husband's voice mail. I left him a message that he had to page me to a good number where I could call him, not his pager because I was calling from a pay phone that didn't accept incoming calls. As I was waiting I began to notice where I was. This was the area that I had been in during the LA riots. I noticed that the old, dilapidated buildings which had burned down had been replaced by new ones, and it was still a dive. God I hate LA. In my nervousness I began to laugh. I thought of how funny it is that the LA Riots were really a "Controlled Burn." My laughter soon turned into tears. I began sobbing. I was sure something else awful had happened. I then saw a marked unit. I flagged him down, and sure enough he had a cell phone. I called my husband again, and paged him to the cell phone.

While we were waiting, the officer began asking me about Customs, and indicated that he was interested in becoming an agent. I was tying his unit up so I felt obligated to give him information about our agency and how to apply. Ironically, I had been the office recruiter for Customs. I took his business card, and told him I would send him the applications that he needed to apply. I knew I would never send them. No one should be recruited into this agency, no one. My husband never called, so I proceeded to our attorney's office. Upon my arrival to the attorney's office, my pager went off. It was my husband calling me from home. I immediately jumped on the phone in the lobby and called home. My husband told me that the 911 page was because I had screwed up the kid's bus passes. This was not my idea of what a 911 page was to be used for. I screamed at him as I described what he had just put me through. Then I slammed the phone down in his ear. For the second time today I had blown up at someone who cares about me. I felt sick.

Sandy and I met with our attorneys. We discuss strategy, and at one point I totally lost it. The stress hit me like a brick wall, and I began sobbing again. Stan, our attorney's assistant, and Sandy did everything they could to make me feel better. The fact that I broke down made our attorney seem very uncomfortable. I had been the strong one through all of this. I'm the one that chose to be vocal and to name Brinkley, by name, in my earlier EEO filings. I'm the one that talked everyone else into filing complaints and taught them how to be tough. Now our attorney's "quarterback" was falling apart. I could feel him squirming in his skin. It made me feel weak and small. Our attorney left, and the rest of us continued the conversation. I kept thinking of how all of this was going to affect my kids and my parents. My parents were almost in their

80s and not in good health. This type of scandal with me in the middle could just kill them. I shared these concerns with Stan and Sandy.

Before I left our attorney's office, I called my husband and apologized. He apologized too and told me to hang in there and that he was with me no matter what happened. When I told this to Stan, he reminded me of how lucky I was. He was right.

On the way home, I began nodding off at the wheel. I was so tired. I pulled over at a mall off of the I-10 freeway and dozed. I began to dream, and suddenly I was at some type of black tie gala, at what appeared to be the Shrine Auditorium in LA. I was standing in a large beautiful foyer, and I saw the toddler outside at the entryway. He looked the same, came into the building, and walked past me smiling. I followed him to a stairwell overlooking the large theater. There were hundreds of people there all in formal attire. I noticed several famous people, Angie Dickinson, Gina Davis, Kevin Costner, and Jay Leno, just to name a few.

I looked down at the toddler and thought to him (as though somehow I knew that he could read my thoughts) why have you brought me here? I don't want to be here. I want to go to the beautiful farm and see who that man is. He looked at me with his beautiful entrancing eyes, and nodded his head towards the edge of the stage. I began looking at the people there, and I noticed that one particular guy stood out to me. His back was to me, and as I began watching him I knew it was the same young man that I had seen at the farm in my other dream. He had on a black tuxedo and held something in his hand. I walked down the steps toward him, trying to see his face. As I walked past the well-dressed people an uncomfortable feeling waved over me. I felt like I didn't belong here with these people, like I was caught eaves dropping on someone's conversation, like a fish out of water. I got as close as I could to the man before the toddler stopped me.

As I watched the young man from behind, I noticed that several people came up to him and shook his hand, or gave him that shallow

Hollywood kiss, common among rich socialites. I noticed that he didn't seem particularly comfortable with this, but was polite and dignified. He stood there alone, only having brief conversations with people. He seemed very stiff, and uncomfortable with his tux. His hands mostly stayed folded together in front of his groin area. His index finger twitched up and down. I could tell that he was just making a necessary appearance here, and that he was going to escape as soon as he had the chance. I noticed that he had folded in his hand, a squeezed pack of cigarettes. I began to hear his soft, deep voice with the Australian or British accent. I wondered if his voice sounded like that because he smoked too much for too long. I tried to move in a position to see his face, but I couldn't. Suddenly, he shifted his weight and slightly turned his head so that I got a glimpse of his left eye. The color of his eye took me by surprise. His eyes were the same beautiful deep, blue as the toddler's. I only noticed his eye for a split second and didn't get to grasp the glimpse that I got of his face, but again I knew that this was a stranger to me. A stranger that I felt some sort of connection to. I received some sort of comfort from him being in my dream. This connection was not in any way romantic, but still somehow, comforting and heart-warming.

I awoke from the dream with my mind racing with questions, and I began to drive home. Why was I at the Shrine Auditorium? I remembered that I had been at the Shrine Auditorium working the Bill and Hillary Clinton campaign as a cross-designated Secret Service Agent. A cross-designated Secret Service Agent is an agent from another Treasury agency (i.e. Customs, IRS, ATF) that has received Secret Service training, and can be used to perform personal protection for the Secret Service. Every four years for the Presidential campaigns and for other manpower intensive events, these cross-designated agents are called upon to augment the Secret Service. I remembered seeing those same movie stars at this and other fund-raisers in Hollywood and Beverly Hills during the campaign. I remembered the highlight of that campaign was when my hero Angie Dickinson shook my hand, and asked me how I liked being an agent. I shyly tipped my head down and said, "Fine, Ma'am." She looked me in the eyes and said, "Myyyyyy, you're a pretty one; you're in the wrong line of work sweetie." That was one of the most special moments in my life, one I'll never forget. When I was little, I use to pretend that I was a policewoman like Angie Dickinson and here I was shaking her hand and being complimented by her. She was gorgeous, and I only hope that I look half that good when I become her age.

My thoughts went back to my dream, and I wondered if my work with the Secret Service during the campaigns had some connection to all of this. I didn't remember anyone looking like this man in my dreams at any of the sites on any of the campaigns. Why was this man there when he clearly didn't want to be there? Maybe his profession required him to be there, in the same way that mine did. Maybe he really wanted to be back at his beautiful farm with his cows, dogs, and ducks, just as much as I did. Why did the toddler take me there? Who was this guy? I tried and tried to recall any features about his face, but all that stood out in my mind were his beautiful blue eyes. Maybe he was the angel of death, and the toddler was my guardian angel. Maybe I was losing my mind.

Chapter 16

The Other Side of The Lens

September 11, 1998, Ruben and I met at the shooting range. Going there actually helped me take my mind off of things. I imagined that the targets were Brinkley, Evantie and Winkowsky. I shot a 148 out of 150, the best I ever shot. After the range, Ruben told me that he wanted me to go by his house and show me something. He also asked Mike Conner to go and whispered to me that he needed an unbiased witness. I then realized that something else had happened. We caravanned over to Ruben's house in Yucaipa. As we were turning down his street, Ruben pointed out the window and at the streetlights. I looked and couldn't believe what I was seeing. There were two cameras, not one but two, on two separate poles, covering both regresses to Ruben's house. Ruben, Mike and I got out and photographed the pole cameras. Mike was extremely surprised and commented that who ever put up these cameras should have notified Ruben that they were watching a crook in his neighborhood. Ruben looked at me and smiled. Then he broke the news to Mike that the pole cameras were for him. Mike became very uncomfortable, yet surprisingly supportive. Mike was the pilot who turned my ex-boyfriend into IA for displaying my pictures. I thought of how ironic it was that here he is now becoming an unwitting witness to our lawsuits. Life is certainly full of strange, intertwined relationships between people. I was sure that when I got home my lights would have cameras as well.

Ruben and I went back to the office and checked in. We then walked to a pay phone close by. For the first time it dawned on us that our phones are probably being monitored also. I felt as though someone had broken into my home and stolen some important possession. In a way that was accurate. They were stealing our privacy, and our lives away from us. Ruben and I called the postal inspector Alexander Pierce regarding the threatening letter and explained everything that was happening to us. We were concerned that Pierce would think that we were just a couple of paranoid nuts. But he didn't. I felt that he really believed us. We called our attorney, but he wasn't in.

Our walk back to the office was full of tension and anguish. We agreed that our phones at home and at work were probably tapped also. Ruben was laughing on the outside, but I could tell that this was all starting to get to him too. Our armor was starting to show chinks, and I began to try to control my fear and focus. That night, I had no cameras at my house that I could see.

On the morning of September 14, I got a strange call from our "favorite" IA investigator Terri Clay, who paged me to his cellular phone. I didn't recognize the number and was very curious when I returned his call. When Mr. Clay answered the phone, I became very angry. Still, I noticed that his tone of voice was very different from all of the other times. He seemed almost meek and practically begged me to meet with him. All of the other times that he called me and asked me to meet with him, he had this almost arrogant, accusing tone of voice which was very different from the meek tone of voice that I was listening to now.

I asked him, "What is this about Terri?" He immediately stated, as if to put me to ease, "This isn't about you, I mean, you're not under investigation." I then responded, "I'm not meeting with you until I know what this is about. My attorney advised me not to go along with any more of your witch-hunts." He replied, "This is about something you may have heard someone say; something someone may have told you."

Darlene and Ruben Sandoval at the firing range

Darlene Qualifying with shotgun at firing range

I thought, oh, now that really clears things up for me. Still, my curiosity got the better of me. So I asked him where he wanted to meet. He said that he would drive out to Riverside and meet me someplace close to my office. Now this was a change. I have always had to drive to Long Beach to the IA office for their inquisitions; they have never offered to drive out here. This peaked my curiosity even more. Clay further pleaded with me to not tell any of my coworkers about this meeting. He told me that he would explain why at our meeting.

On Wednesday September 16th, I agreed to meet with IA Clay for lunch. I didn't trust IA or what the real purpose of this meeting was, so I did tell Ruben Sandoval about this meeting. Ruben was going to set up in his car across the street, and I asked my long time friend and hairdresser Roberta Rossa to be inside the restaurant to witness the meeting. Roberta was the only hairdresser in my whole life who listened to how you wanted your hair and did it right. She was also one of the smartest gals that I'd ever met. She would have made a great agent.

We met at a restaurant called Spoons next to our office. When I walked in I saw Roberta in the front by the bar area, and I saw Mr. Clay in the back towards the window. Roberta smiled at me as if to say, don't worry, I got you covered. Roberta is extremely sharp and one of the few people that I can really trust. Even though she was not in law enforcement, I knew that instinctively she knew what to do. There are three professions that seem to have a sixth sense of human behavior, and that's cops, shrinks, and hairdressers.

As I sat down at the table, I noticed that Mr. Clay had selected a seat right next to the front window, a tactic commonly used by cops when someone outside is covering them. I was chuckling inside about the situation. Here we were, both with someone covering us, and both pretending to be meeting alone. What a joke. As I sat down I gave him a condescending combination smirk and headshake, as if to let him know what a jerk I thought he was. I said, "O.K. Clay, what's this all about?" He began by thanking me for meeting him alone and that he didn't want any of my coworkers to know that he was meeting with me. He then stated that he and his boss believed that their office (IA) was being used by someone in my office to harm me. I was thinking to myself, no shit Sherlock. What a rocket scientist I'm dealing with here. He then showed me a transcript that someone had typed and mailed into their office anonymously. The transcript was constructed as though it were of a tape-recorded conversation between someone at the air unit and me speaking about information on my ex-boyfriend. The transcript had the signature block of our Investigative Aid, Yolanda Rios. There was no signature, just her signature block. As I read this, I felt the rage rising up through me. I knew that I had to conceal this, just in case this was another of IA's stunts to get me to over-react, and do something unprofessional.

I told Clay that this was bogus and that this conversation never happened. Clay stated that their office was worried that someone had been illegally wire tapping my phone because of the way the transcript was written. I then clarified for him that I believed that this was written by someone who knew that I had a court order and restraining orders allowing me to record conversations between my ex-boyfriend and I because of his previous threatening phone calls. This transcript was written to make it appear as though I was illegally recording people not covered in my court order as well. It became immediately apparent to me that Einstein Clay hadn't figured this out yet, and only when I pointed out the obvious did the moron get it. These are the type of agents that go to IA. Serving a term in IA is the only way these mediocre agents would ever get a promotion otherwise.

I then expressed my feelings of controlled rage that this was being done to me. I told him of my letter of disciplinary action. I quoted the last paragraph of this letter stating, "if circumstances change, this letter may be removed from your personnel file by local management." He reacted by rolling his eyes and shaking his head in disbelief that someone was stupid enough to put this type of language in a letter such as

this. Again, Clay expressed that "for what ever reason, someone was trying to"...and I then finished the sentence for him..."Screw with me,"
and he nodded his head yes. I starred into his eyes to see if he would
break eye contact with me and turn his head (a body language cue to
someone's insincerity). He kept good eye contact as I tried to read him
and seemed surprisingly sincere.

I then made a suggestion to him: that he shouldn't be meeting with
me alone anymore. If he was in fact uninvolved in all of this, and that he
was just being caught in the middle as he had indicated; that he should
ask to be removed from investigating me anymore. I suggested that the
next time he is asked to investigate Ruben, Sandy, or myself, (all of
which have law-suits pending) to just try to get out of it and see what
happens. He gave me a funny look, as if to say, "I don't get it." I told him
to think about it.

As we were walking out, two people who I know were sitting in the
bar area. They smiled and waved at me. They were the people who
owned the 76 station where I always took my G-Ride in for an oil and
lube change. I waved back, and noticed that Mr. Clay was giving me a
funny look. I could tell that he was assuming that I had asked these people to cover this meeting, and that I wanted him to know that they were
there; that I had witnesses. I began to chuckle. I thought it ironic that he
was drawing the correct conclusion about the wrong people. If he only
knew that it was Roberta and not they. Oh well!

On September 16, 1998, all SAIC, RAIC, and Supervisor personnel
from the SAIC/LA and the SAIC/San Diego were mandated to attend a
management conference, held in the Palm Springs area. The main topic
for discussion was a class entitled "Dealing with Problem Employees." A
private attorney, and former employee of the U.S. Customs Office of
Regional Council taught this class. My good friend and excellent
Customs manager Ricardo Sandoval attended this conference.

When he got back from the conference, Ricardo briefed Sandy and I,
via the phone. He told us that Lawrence Evantie cut him down in front

of everybody, and they exchanged verbal digs. I could tell that Ricardo really hated Evantie and wondered what Evantie's problem was. I explained to him that Evantie was doing management's dirty work for them. Evantie is one of Brinkley's stooges. I explained that Evantie was trying to give everyone the perception that the RAIC/RV (our Riverside Office) and Ricardo's office, RAIC/Calexico, weren't getting along because of how Ricardo was handling things. Evantie was purposely undermining the relationship between the two offices in an effort to make Ricardo look bad. Ricardo and Sandy agreed that I was probably right in my assessment.

I thought about just how amazing it was that a hand-full of people, or even one person, could falsely alter the perceptions of others about someone they wanted to undermine. I had heard so many stupid rumors about Ricardo Sandoval, and of how he only got his promotion because he filed a lawsuit, and that he was incompetent. This was all a crock of shit. I remembered about how I had heard so much negative gossip about Hillary Clinton, when Bill was first running for office, and subsequently continuing after. I had heard from dozens of men about how she was a real "ball buster", and of how these people had heard from "THEM" that she was a bitch to Secret Service Agents, and a real political climber. Of course these rumors always came from the "THEM" zone; you know those mythological people who disperse information that conveniently fits the agenda of the person spreading the gossip. I was a "die-hard" Republican (Ronald Reagan was my hero), and there was a part of me that very stupidly believed in all of this gossip, because it comfortably aligned with my political beliefs.

Then I was fortunate to be assigned to protect Hillary Clinton as an adjunct Treasury agent or OTA (Other Treasury Agents Assigned), during Bills first and second campaign. I was amazed. After every negative thing that I had heard about Hillary, what I saw with my own two eyes highly disturbed me. I wasn't assigned directly to her jump team, but I did have the opportunity to observe her numerous times in, and out of the eye of the public. She was nothing like what all of these men, and the obvious male chauvinists in the "THEY ZONE" had described. She was this very professional, demure, and soft-spoken little petite woman. She was always warm and friendly toward the Treasury agents, and not once did I see her acting in any way like a ball-busting bitch. She spent a lot of time working very hard on health care issues with her staff, and seemed very sincere about her work. My dad always taught me that right, wrong, or indifferent, people will judge you by the company you keep. Well, I had the opportunity to communicate frequently with members Hillary's staff, which were mostly female. They too were very nice, warm, professional ladies, who never came off as bitchy, or over-barring. Hillary kept good company, and I was surprisingly impressed. I learned something very important from this, and from Ricardo's situation: the "THEY's" of the world use gossip to undermine people that they are afraid of. It is a subversive, cowardly tool to enhance the perpetrator's agenda. It is a tool that I would never fall for again.

My attention then turned back to our three-way conversation, and Sandy, Ricardo, and I, shared feelings of how the stress of the retaliation that we had all received was affecting our lives, at home and at work. Ricardo began confiding in us that he went to the gym almost every night in the same way that I did; only he lifted weights. We shared with each other how it was impacting our marriages, and causing stress on our families. The conversation strayed to the dangers of this job and how all of this stuff was in many ways more stressful than the times that he and I were almost blown away. I thought about my strange dreams, and I asked him if he believed in guardian angels. I was surprised with the following story that Ricardo shared with us:

Ricardo was working a dope deal, deep undercover south of the border in Tijuana (TJ). The deal went south (cop slang for a deal going bad), and the crooks thought that Ricardo was trying to rip them off. They kidnapped him, and somehow he convinced them that he was about to get a large sum of money. They only had to take him into TJ,

Darlene with President Reagan

and his girlfriend would get the money. This was all a lie, and Ricardo was just trying to stall for time any way he could to stay alive until the surveillance team found them. Ricardo was wired up during this whole thing. The crooks took him into TJ, parked the car in a shopping mall parking lot, and told Ricardo to stay in the car. The crooks exited the car, and left Ricardo alone. All of the sudden, a strange Latin male, not one of the crooks that Ricardo had been dealing with, got into the car and sat next to him. The guy said, "Hey buddy, just calm down. You're going to make it through this, but you got to calm down and clear your head." Rick said that they conversed for several minutes and then the guy got out. Just as the guy got out, federal agents were surrounding the car, the crooks and Rick. The guy had just disappeared, and no one else had seen him. Ricardo didn't know how on earth the guy could have gotten past all of those federal agents with their guns drawn. Sandy asked Ricardo if he had ever listened to the tape of where he was wired. Ricardo answered, "You know, that's the strangest thing, I did; and all you can hear in the conversation is my voice."

I was taken a-back by Ricardo's story. Ricardo is one of the most honest men I've ever met and was not the type to make this kind of thing up or imagine it. I wanted so badly to share my reoccurring dream with him and Sandy, but I lacked the confidence. I was afraid that they would think that I was nuts. Ricardo's story made me much more comfortable with my dreams. Maybe these dreams did mean something, and the toddler and the man were somehow trying to direct or help me.

On September 23, 1998, I got a call from Tom Best, from his UP (Union Pacific Railroad) office. He had profiled a series of five or six tanker cars and was setting them up for weight. I briefed our new Group supervisor O'Shea, and he seemed somewhat enthused. Evantie tried to pull me off the project again, but no one else in the office had the expertise, or the desire to deal with this, so I was back on for now, and it was made clear to me for only a short time. Evantie clearly hated the fact that he had no choice but to put me back in the rail yards, doing my job. Best, Ervin Rios, and I began running all the leads, and pulling all the entry information on the cars. As I began down this long tanker car road again, part of me wanted to put in for sick leave and pawn this mess off on someone else. I wanted to stick it to Evantie the way he had stuck it to me and leave him with no one qualified to control this rail car fiasco. I knew that it wouldn't matter how well I did, how much dope I seized, or how many people I put in jail, I wouldn't get any credit for a job well done, and others less qualified than I would be promoted over me. This was the first time I recall feeling this way about my work. I felt so burnt, but I did my job anyway.

September 25, 1998, the SAC Los Angeles had their annual awards ceremony and picnic at a park in Long Beach. Ruben and I went together, and had agreed to meet Sandy, Paige Yates (our mole under Brinkley's nose at the SAIC office), and the rest of the "Trouble Makers" there. We thought it might be fun for Brinkley to see us all together eating his free food. Just before we left the office for this gala event, I got a call from Chief Inspector Jeremy O'Leary. O'Leary was working on the rail project with me. He and I teamed up because of all of the trouble that I was having tracking railroad cars and their cargo in my two cases, Operation Black Widow, and Operation Tanker Car. O'Leary called with some terrific ideas on how to get funding for the current suspect tanker cars that I was going to have to open on Monday. It cost a lot of money to have a contract company examine these tanker cars. This was the end of the fiscal year for government funding, and the RAC/Riverside was out of money. I liked O'Leary's ideas but had no authority to agree to them. So, I asked O'Leary to talk to my RAC Evantie about extending my stay on the rail project, and he agreed.

As Brinkley was talking to Evantie, Ruben and I left for the picnic. Ruben and I only stayed for about an hour, ate and left. We didn't stay for the awards ceremony, and I'm glad we didn't. Once again, everyone else in my office was recognized for his or her work for the year, and I received nothing. I don't know why I was somewhat surprised. I should have expected it. I guess I thought that the tanker car case was so significant, (the biggest seizure in our office) significant enough for the acting Commissioner of Customs to call me and thank me for all of the work that I was doing on the case, significant enough that Janet Reno was closely watching this case; that I thought that even Brinkley wouldn't be dumb enough to try this stunt, but he did. People in my office that hadn't done "Jack" for years, got recognition for something, and here I had the second most significant case of the year for this entire agency, and I didn't even get honorable mention. My case was only second to Operation Casablanca, an international, undercover, money-laundering operation that, coincidentally, was targeting the same organization that I was targeting in my tanker car case.

Well, Brinkley's stunt had the desired effect; I was crushed. The good news was that he'd never know that this stunt hurt me so. I had several agents, Bob Mattivi, Ruben Sandoval, Sandy Nunn tell me that this was, again, a real slap in the face. Everyone knew the significance of the Tanker Car case and knew that it was a real farce that I received no recognition for it. I came home, cried, called Sam at our attorney's office and relayed the story to him. He tried to console me, in the same way that everyone else did, by saying, "Don't worry, this will only really help your law suit." For some reason this didn't make me feel any better, but I did learn something from this. I now knew just how far my RAC Lawrence Evantie, and SAIC Drake Brinkley would go on this playing field. It was clear that Evantie was actively carrying out Brinkley's plans for us, for it was Evantie's responsibility to put me in for an award, and he didn't. I had the most significant case in the RAC office, and he made a point of ensuring that everyone but me had an award of some type.

Here I was for the last two days dealing with five more tanker cars, supposedly loaded with dope, and Evantie was using my talents, and all the while, he was stabbing me in the back. If that wasn't enough, I then got a call from Ervin Rios. Ervin told me that after Chief O'Leary had his conversation with my boss Evantie earlier that day, O'Leary then called Ervin to relay the gist of the conversation. Evidentially, while O'Leary was attempting to offer help on these tanker cars to Evantie, Evantie was very negative and made it clear that he didn't want Inspection and Control involved. Additionally, Evantie told O'Leary that they were considering taking me off of this case, and that Evantie didn't want me involved in the Operation Lite Rail project. O'Leary tried to reason with Evantie and attempted to explain to him how it was most necessary that I be involved in this project, but this, of course, was to no avail. When O'Leary point blank asked Evantie why I wasn't going to be allowed to participate in Operation Lite Rail and why I was being taken off of the case, Evantie answered, "It's just politics."

What a crock of bull! I was taught in the military that the mission comes first, then your men, then your needs come last. In Customs, managers stick their finger in their mouth, moisten it, and raise their moistened finger in the air to see which way the political wind is blowing before they make a decision. The Customs management philosophy is to decide what political best interest is served first, then how their personal best interest can be served by using the political best interest as their vehicle. Then they consider how the mission might be accomplished without damaging their political best interest, and then the troops, well the troops are simply cannon fader to serve the interest of corrupt managers and their politics.

Chapter 17

Depositions

October 2, 1998, the U.S. Attorney's office in Ruben Sandoval's case deposed me. The U.S. Attorney's office represents U.S. Customs in these civil law suits. The AUSA (Assistant United States Attorney) on this case is an AUSA that used to work in the criminal division. I was under oath being grilled for over eight hours. When it was all over, I had a sense of relief. I felt good that all of their scare tactics failed, and I had done my duty by telling the truth about what happened to Ruben, Sandy, and me. I felt professional again. I felt a sense of cleansing by standing up to adversity with dignity and honor. I told the truth at whatever cost to come.

On October 7, 1998, our attorneys in Ruben's federal case deposed SAIC Brinkley. SAIC Brinkley lied, and denied that he made any statements about dealing with any complaints generated from the RAIC/Riverside during the November 96 promotion party. Additionally, Brinkley stated that he had nothing to do with the assignment of vehicles to agents.

On October 7, 1998, our attorneys in Ruben's federal case also deposed SSA Peter Blake. In this deposition Blake confirmed that he had attended this promotion party and that Brinkley did in fact make the comments about dealing with complainants at the RAIC/RV. When asked about the incident of he and Edwin Easel taking heroin home overnight, Blake lied under oath and denied this accusation.

On October 9, 1998, Ruben and I were loaned out to RAIC/Orange County (RAIC/OC) for a series of search warrants. When we arrived at

RAIC/OC that morning for the briefing, Peter Blake was the case agent delivering the briefing. When we walked in to the room there were already about 30 agents and TFO's (task force officers) present. Ruben grabbed a donut and some coffee, and we sat down. Blake looked up and saw Ruben and I glaring at him disapprovingly. In fact, if looks could kill, he'd be dead. I thought to myself, what a little lying weasel. Blake quickly broke eye contact, and his face turned red with embarrassment. I said under my breath, "COWARD." Ruben kicked me in the shins under the table and said to me, "SSSHHHH, Hothead."

On our way home from executing these warrants, we hit typical Southern California rush hour traffic. Ruben and I got a chance to brainstorm. We were so pissed off that Blake had committed perjury and would probably get away with it. I asked Ruben if he was still alternate evidence custodian, and he said he was. I asked him if he could get into the evidence locker tonight and look at the logs. He stated that he really wasn't supposed to be in there without the authority of the primary evidence custodian David Gray. I asked him if he'd ever looked at the logs to see if they failed to cover their tracks on the taking heroin home. Ruben said, "No, but nobody's that dumb Dar. You know they covered themselves in the logs." I told Ruben, "Dude, don't underestimate how dumb these people really are." After some convincing, Ruben and I proceeded to the RAIC/RV and entered the evidence room. Much to Ruben's surprise, the log clearly showed that the heroin didn't go back to the evidence room until the evening of the next day. As Ruben and I high-fived each other, I said, "I told you so homey."

Ruben and I immediately entered the file room and photocopied the evidence log. As Ruben was doing this, I pulled SA Janet Sommer's case file on this heroin case and found her 9-B's (case chronology form) where she had briefed Winkowsky on the heroin going home with Easel and of her concerns for her criminal case. I photocopied these too. We then picked up the phone and contacted the on call IA duty agent and reported this. Ruben faxed the logs to him, and we both could smell justice in the air, and I could see joy on Ruben's face. I slept well that night, and had no memorable dreams or stomach burn.

On October 13, 1998, our attorneys in Ruben's federal lawsuit deposed SSA Jerry Johnston. During the deposition Jerry Johnston was asked the following question, "Did Supervisor Ivan Winkowsky have a problem with women in law enforcement?" Before he could answer this question, the AUSA representing Customs (Tim Deer) stopped the deposition and asked Jerry to step outside. Jerry and Deer stepped into the hall where Deer directed Jerry not to answer that question. Jerry was a prior Military Officer, a fellow Kentuckian, and a very honorable agent. He looked at Deer in disbelief and went back into the deposition. Our attorney asked Jerry the question again, and Jerry in a very clear, and determined tone of voice, told the truth that Winkowsky did have a problem with women.

On October 13, 1998, AUSA Deer issued a letter, which was essentially a gag order, to U.S. Customs. This letter was directed to all U.S. Customs employees specifically regarding SA Sandoval's civil litigation against Customs. This memo was sent by facsimile and federal express. It was addressed to SAIC Drake Brinkley. The memo directed Customs management to, "Please advise your employees accordingly." I had a mole at the SAIC office right under Brinkley's nose that got me a copy of this document. There's a word for Mr. Deer's behavior, it's called witness tampering.

The next day, Jerry Johnston told me about his deposition and what had happened. I could tell that it was important to him that I knew that he did the right thing and told the truth. I gave him a hug and said, "Was there ever any doubt? Well done my Kentucky Pizanno." Jerry and I had very similar, almost parallel lives. We were both military officers, we were from Kentucky, and somehow ended up in the same office together. Jerry's integrity was firmly intact, and I knew that he would say the right thing under pressure. I was proud of him.

On October 14, 1998, ASAIC (Assistant Special Agent In Charge) Donald Chin, under oath, during deposition, confirmed suspicions that pre-selection (a practice against OPM regulations) was definitely involved in the selection process of late 1996, where Ruben and I were passed over. On most everything else, Chin played dumb. Chin worked directly under Brinkley, and to no one's surprise, he retired shortly after this deposition.

On November 10, 1998, Ruben Sandoval sent a letter to the Customs Commissioner, Raymond Kelly, regarding the lack of investigation by IA into the mishandling of evidence (heroin), and subsequent cover up. We were sure that Kelly would either ignore it completely, or simply sick his IA dogs on us again. Either way, we wanted to ensure that we documented that he was in fact informed, and can't play ignorant sometime down the road.

On December 9, 1998, the Director of the Office of Internal Affairs, Harrison Wells, notified SA Sandoval that his office would not be investigating this matter. His letter stated that IA cannot investigate itself and that the investigation would be referred to the U.S. Treasury Department, Office of the Inspector General (commonly referred to by most agents as the black hole where everything gets buried and nothing gets done). Harrison Wells was himself currently being investigated by a grand jury on corruption charges brought against him related to the whistle blowing of RAIC/Calexico, Ricardo Sandoval. Drake Brinkley placed Harrison Wells in the position of Director of IA, when Brinkley was the Director of the Customs Office of Investigations (the Special Agents). I guess it takes a crook to promote a crook.

Chapter 18

Wake Up and Smell The Corruption

On January 17, 1999, I got a call from Tom Best, UP (Union Pacific) Railroad. He told me that he had five more tanker cars sitting in his yard, manifested and empty, and all of them were five to nine tons over weight. I told him that I was taken off of the rail project. He said, "Well who in the hell am I supposed to call? Nobody else over there knows this stuff, and I don't want to talk to any one else." I replied, "All right Tom, what's the numbers?" He gave me the car numbers, and I pulled the entries from the Customs Computers. Just as I feared, the Customs general hold that I had previously placed in the system had already been released. If it weren't for the alertness of Tom Best, the cars would have never been brought back to the Colton rail yard.

Bob Mattivi was the acting group supervisor at the time. Bob was a super agent. He had made some of the most famous cases in Customs and was certainly my mentor when I first came on the job. I trusted Bob, and decided to show him what we had found on the tanker cars. I called Best back, and asked him to bring the routes of the cars (print outs from the UP computer system displaying the routes of rail cars after they entered the U.S.). When Best arrived, we looked at the routes of these cars. The rout was very suspicious. On the manifest, these cars were manifested as empty. Railroads invoice their customers by weight, and distance; therefore making it more cost effective for the customer to route their cars in the most direct manner possible. These cars were imported from Baja, Mexico, routed through Texas and Arizona, and then sent to Colton, California. This made no sense, and would not be cost effective for the shipper/customer. The manifest also had stamped on it, "NO WEIGHT PER WEIGH AGREEMENT." Shippers will often have a standing account set up with the major railroads and are invoiced to their credit line. The accounts can be set up to prepay the routs, at the max cost, assuming the weight will be at the maximum. This saves the shipper the expense of having to pay the route (distance) cost of having the cars sent to a weight location to be weighed. When this occurs, the manifest will be stamped "NO WEIGHT PER WEIGH AGREEMENT." This method is not, however, normally done for empty cars (why would you prepay for a full car when the car is empty) and never on pressurized tanker cars. Tanker cars, due to my rail project and Customs holds have to be shipped to a weigh station anyway, and the shipper eats the cost of the extra distance as the price of doing business compliments of the U.S. Customs Service.

The way these cars were routed and manifested made no sense. Best and I briefed Mattivi. Mattivi seemed pleased and said, "Well Dar, it looks like you guys may have gotten yourself another big load. Let me go brief Evantie and," I interrupted Mattivi and said, "Wow Bob. Before you go up there, there's something you should know. I don't want you to get blind sided with anything. Bob, Evantie jerked me of the rail project, and told me to stay away from there. If you go in there with this, Evantie's going to throw a fit." Bob looked at me like I was crazy and said, "Oh now Darlene; no he won't. You're just being sensitive because of all the bullshit that you and Ruben are going through. Besides, who else am I going to send? Everyone else is in training, and you're the only one that knows this stuff." He smiled at me with his sweet, wise, all knowing face, as if to say, "Just trust your old mentor," and he took the documentation, and walked to Evantie's office.

After a few seconds, Best and I heard Evantie yelling at Bob. Several minutes later, Mattivi returned to the back of the office where we were waiting for him. He tossed the documents down on the table in front of us in disgust. He sat down, looked at Best with this bewildered look, and said, "I don't know what to say. I don't know what to tell you guys. He wouldn't even entertain us having them pressure tested at no cost to the government. This is ridiculous."

I had been sitting there leaning back with my feet propped up on the table and drinking a bottle of Arrowhead water. I brought my feet to the floor, tossed my water bottle in the trash in disgust, and asked, "Now do you believe me Bob?" Mattivi answered, "I don't know what to believe, and I'm embarrassed to say this, but Darlene stay away from this." I could tell by the look of anguish on his face that Bob was concerned for me, disturbed by Evantie's reaction, and totally stumped as to what to do. This was the first time I had seen Mattivi at a loss for a quick-witted answer. Mattivi was a sharp, confident, seasoned veteran who was never at a loss for what to do. His reaction scared me. I got up and walked Best to his car. When we got to Best's car, he questioned me "What's going on here Darlene? Is someone corrupt here or what?" I shook my head in embarrassment and disgust, looked down at the ground, and said, "Best, you know it isn't me dude." Best replied, "No, I know it isn't you Dar. You're the only one that I've been able to deal with over here; But something about this just doesn't look right Darlene, and you know it." I looked up at him and said, "Best, I don't know what to do." He took mercy on me, shook my hand, and ended the conversation by saying, "Hey, we'll have to get together and talk about this later." Five days later, the tanker cars were released without so much as even a pressure test being done, which would have been at no cost to the government. Five suspect pressurized tanker cars five to nine tons over weight, manifested as empty were released against policy and made it to their destination, a rail spur, somewhere in downtown LA. With all of the indicators/red flags that we had, those cars should have never been released without at least being pressure tested.

I met Ruben and Renado the day the cars were released and told them what had happened. Renado couldn't believe it. "Darlene, this shit is getting dangerous. I'm telling you, I've said it once and I'll say it again, this stuff has nothing to do with this EEO crap you guys are dealing with. I think you've wandered into some serious corruption in your agency, and that Brinkley guy is in it up to his nose. Or maybe it's some type of CIA undercover shit or something." Renado began looking around in an animated, paranoid fashion as if he were looking for somebody about to get him and said jokingly, "Gees! I'm gonna get the hell away from you guys, the red dot could appear on your forehead any minute." We all laughed, and I said, "Yeah, there you go again, that YOU GUYS shit. Renado face it, you're in this dude." Renado responded, "Oh no I'm not." He pulled out his badge and pointed at it and said, "You see this here, it says San Bernardino Police Department, not Department of Treasury." Then I pulled out my badge pointed at it and said, "Oh, you mean U.S. Corruptions." We all busted a gut laughing and when the laughter stopped, I could see the concern on their faces.

I knew Renado was just kidding us. I knew that Renado would never let us down. The man knew what the word loyalty meant. I thought of how Renado reminded me so much of one of my NCOIC's (Non Commissioned Officers In Charge) in the military. His name was William Watson, but we called him Little Willie for short. Little Willie was 6ft 3in, and weighed about 300lbs of pure muscle (similar to Renado's build, but only taller). I remembered one time when I was a young Lieutenant and I was duty officer. I got a call in the middle of the night from one of my M.P.'s (Military Police), in a very panicked voice over the radio, "Hey L.T. (short for Lieutenant); You better get out here. We got a wild man, I need help." I jumped into the car with Willie and he sped out to the west gate of the post, out in the middle of nowhere.

When we arrived, there were two marked units, and four of my M.P.'s were surrounding the guy who was acting crazy. We got out of the unit, and one of the M.P.'s ran over to us. I asked, "What's going on; what's this guy's problem?" The M.P. was out of breath and his wired rimmed glasses had been smashed on his face. He caught his breath and said, "I'm not sure L.T., but I think this guy has rabies." "Rabies!" I exclaimed.

We had been having a rabies epidemic on the post that summer. There had been several rabid skunks, squirrels, and even domestic cats killed by animal control. They had been giving out warnings for the past several weeks about having your pets inoculated, the warning signs of rabies, and other precautions. I looked at the guy and sure enough, he was foaming at the mouth, swatting at everyone, and growling at them like a mad man. The M.P. showed me that he had already broken through two sets of handcuffs and put bite marks in my M.P.'s Cochran jump boots. I realized that if this guy bit, scratched or slobbered on us we would have to get those God-forsaken rabies shots, and even those weren't 100% effective. Willie looked at me and said, "L.T., we can't risk the lives of our men. We're gonna have to shoot this guy. L.T., rabies is potentially fatal, and this is a life threatening situation that calls for deadly force." When he said this, my face dropped. I was only a whopping 23 years old. I knew when I entered law enforcement that someday I might be faced with having to kill someone, but this was not how I pictured it.

Willie saw the terrified look on my face and laughed. He walked to the rear of his car and said, "Don't worry LT. I got you covered." He pulled a tire iron out of his trunk and walked over to me and the other M.P. He said, "I need you two to distract him from the front, so I can get a wack at him from the back." The M.P. and I pulled our nightsticks, and began distracting him from the front. We would poke at him with the sticks from a safe distance, and he would lunge at us. Willie was working his way around him when the mad man lunged at me, and I fell backwards over a rock. The man ran at me and I could see his evil, crazed looking eyes as he was ready to pounce on me. It was one of the most horrific things I can ever remember seeing. Just as the lunatic was on top of me, Willie cracked his scull with the tire iron. He dropped down almost on top of me, and slobber dripped from his mouth on to my uniform. I jumped up in terror, ran to my vehicle, grabbed a piece of

Darlene conducting training as Captain in the U.S. Army M.P. Corps

Darlene teaching water survival in the Army

cloth lying on the seat, and desperately wiped the slobber off. The next day, we found out that the mad man didn't have rabies, but was on PCP. When I was told this, my heart dropped. I thought, my God, I almost ordered this man executed, and he didn't have rabies. I will always remember Willie's quick thinking, and be grateful for him saving my ass. I had the same kind of warm fuzzy loyalty about Renado. Renado had saved Ruben's and my butts more times than I can count.

On February 8, 1999, I was out on surveillance when I got a 911 page from Ruben. I knew this was serious; if Ruben puts in 911, it's serious. I cell phoned him, and he told me that he was called into Lewis' office, and was informed that tomorrow morning that he had to drive to San Diego to be interviewed by Internal Affairs. Ruben tried to make his voice sound confident, but I could sense the fear and anger in him. He asked me if I could meet him and Renado for lunch, and I did.

We met at this little hole in the wall Mexican food place that Renado and Ruben liked. It's a real low-key place, and not likely to bump into any IA pukes. Renado greeted me with his usual bear hug, and Ruben looked depressed, and worried. When I shook his hand he squeezed my hand hard and stared deeply into my eyes, as though he was trying to transmit his pain to me through a sense of tough. I shook my head and uttered a stream of cuss words. Ruben said, "Renado, can you believe that she kisses our friend Ben with that mouth," to which I replied, "I only get like this around you guys. You're a bad influence," and we all laughed.

Renado just kept shaking his head as we updated him on the latest. He just kept saying, "Darlene, this is about the tanker car case, I'm telling you! You were never supposed to find that dope. You messed up somebody's action. They wouldn't go to these extremes of coming after you guys over an EEO complaint. I'm telling you. You know it, and I know it! This is some serious shit here, and even your prosecutor Yvette is worried. I'm telling you, you guys are in danger, you guys are in danger!" "Wait a minute" I replied. "What do you mean you guys? I seem to recall that you were out there with me, every step of the way amigo, crawling all over those cars. You mean WEEE are in danger." Renado responded, "I don't think so little missy, there aren't any IA investigations or surveillance on me; not yet anyways." Renado's laughter faded, and I could see the fear on his face as he continued, "I'm telling you, what you guys put together with Rios paints a very scary picture. This isn't just about your EEO fight. You stumbled right into a shit-storm. You picked up a rock that you weren't supposed to see under." As I thought about what Renado said, I felt a burning sensation in my stomach. I wasn't sure if it was from the fear of what I had gotten us into, or the incredibly bad food Ruben keeps making me eat at this little hole in the wall. I swam a mile in 57 minutes, and ran three miles that evening before I went home to my kids. I can't take this anger home with me, my family deserves better than this.

That night when I got home my husband Ben remarked, "You were at the gym for a long time. What happened at work today?" I told Ben what happened and what Renado thinks concerning the situation. I saw fear on my husband's face. Ben said in a low serious voice, "I want you, Sandy and Ruben to quit digging into this tanker car crap." Ben's fear turned quickly to anger when I didn't respond. Ben grabbed my shoulders, looked me dead in the eye and said, "What are you crazy? You're going to get us all killed! I saw on the news what they did to those people in Matamoras, (referring to the 1999 slaying of the 21 men, women, and children murdered in Matamoras, Mexico by suspected members of the Arellano-Felix Drug Cartel) and that's the same organization you're going after!" I broke away from him and explained, "What the hell do you expect me to do? This is my job!" Ben responded, "Not that part isn't. Not that in-house corruption that you all are going after. Look, just do your criminal case, and leave the other stuff alone, please, Darlene, please. Our kids need their mom, and Ruben's kids need him, and Sandy needs... well, Sandy needs to get laid." Ben looked at me and smiled. I smiled back. At dinner, Ben looked at all of the kids and then looked at me and said, "This is what's important sweety, this."

On February 9, 1999, Ruben made his journey to San Diego. I tried to go with him, but he wouldn't let me. This was his attempt at showing some kind of control over the situation. When I went into the office I passed by that little snake Edwin Easel. He had this little arrogant smirk on his face as if to say, "HA, HA, Ruben's getting his now isn't he, and you're next." As he walked past me with that smirk I said, "Well girly boy, did your kids pick out your wardrobe today? That's some gay shirt you got on there." This was my weak attempt at wiping the sneer off his little face without hitting him upside the head with my tennis racket (kept in office for play at lunch). Easel replied with, "HA, HA, HA, how mature of you Darlene." I responded, "Fuck you weasel, you little ass kissing, pischer. Why don't you run into Evantie's office and kiss his butt. Maybe he'll spoon-feed you another case." Yolanda (our office Investigative Aid) saved me by interrupting and saying, "Hey, both of you pipe down right now or I'll kick both of your asses." I knew not to tangle with Yolanda. Yolanda is a New York Puerto Rican that could kick both of our butts. Yolanda was my friend, an incredibly sharp lady who had her integrity in the right place. She knew what had been going on with all of this bullcrap and she resented it. She too had demonstrated a spine, and when it came time for her to be interviewed by the EEO and IA investigators, she came forward and told the truth at great risk. I was grateful for her courage, and I was grateful to her for the save between Easel the weasel, and me.

I went into the kitchen and got a Dew. I couldn't sleep the night before. I was worried, and pissed off about what was going to happen to Ruben. I can always count on Mt. Dew to keep me on the go and awake. I passed Yolanda in the hall and she pulled me back into the kitchen and asked, "A Mt. Dew this early in the morning, and taking on Easel the Weasel, what's going on Darlene?" I briefed her, and you could see the concern on her face for me. She put her arm around me and said,

"Listen girlfriend, you got to not react to this stuff. This little episode in the hall here is just what they want. They know you have a temper, and they are using Ruben and Sandy to get to you. They ain't got nothing on you they can come after you with, so they are pushing your buttons. Just chill lady, just chill." I gave Yolanda a big hug, thanked her for the good advice, and headed back to my office. As I drank my Dew, my stomach felt like someone was stabbing me with a burning, hot knife. It felt like I had taken a shot of whiskey, and I could feel it burn all the way down my throat; I wanted to vomit.

I made a weak attempt at completing some reports, but I kept making a lot of mistakes. I was tired from lack of sleep, worried and anxious because I hadn't heard from Ruben, and sick to my stomach from the stress and the Dew. I completed some packing in the office. We were moving our office from the northeastern part of the City of Riverside, to Downtown Riverside close to the courthouse. We had been loading a moving van all day long, and currying things over to the new office. Most of us were pretty sad to leave this old office. We had a lot of good times there, and a lot of great memories. At lunchtime, we all went to the back and had a little celebration to say good-by to the old office. There were a couple of bottles of wine involved, and a lot of good food. I, of course, had my husband "Chef Ben" prepare something fabulous.

As the afternoon grew, I took special note that one of our more decadent/loose agents Sherry King was getting plastered with David Gray. Sherry was the kind of female agent that does more damage to the reputation of women in the work place, than does most male chauvinists men. Sherry had an affair with one of our former RAIC's (Resident Agent In Charge / the boss of our field office) Jim Wilson, and everyone knew about it. They weren't exactly what you would call discrete. Everyone in the office knew Jim Wilson's wife and liked her. This caused a morale problem in the office, and lessened the credibility of Jim Wilson. Sherry is the type of female that displays this type of behavior on a silver platter, to be used as ammunition by male chauvinists in their broad brushing of all women in the work place.

I noticed that Sherry was not only plastered, but that Gray had then loaded her and her glass of wine in his G-ride, and transported her to the new office. Sherry was so plastered that everyone noticed it, and I'm confident that Evantie new it too. I was also confident that no manager would say anything or report the two of them for their behavior, especially Gray. I found this appalling. Gray was instrumental in going after Ruben for the ridiculous, children in the G-ride incident, yet here Gray was transporting a drunken female agent and her alcohol in his G-ride. What a hypocrite.

As I sat there observing this fiasco and pondering how to handle it, the phone rang. It was Sandy asking if I had heard anything. I told her no. She sensed that I was really worried and she stated, "This is just such fucking bullshit man. The bright side of this is that these morons are just proving our point and making us one hell of a lawsuit. Don't worry Darlene, Ruben's smart, he'll keep his cool, and he will be all right. I'm sure that he'll call us when they're done with him." Sandy's a great gal. She always tries to make me feel better when I need it most. I told her of what I had just observed between Gray and Sherry King. She told me that I should definitely report it to IA, to see if they would lift a finger to go after one of their fellow goons. I knew she was right.

I then warned her again, about that Huge World crap. I told her she better cool it, or she would be giving them phony ammunition to come get her. I also told her about what Ben had said about our extracurricular internal corruption investigation, and about how I'd lost it with Easel the Weasel this morning in the hall. When I got off of the phone with Sandy, I felt bad about causing her more concern, she's got her share of troubles, and doesn't need me to be chastising her. Here she called to be supportive, and all I did was run her down. I felt like such a bitch.

At 1500hours, I gave up on my quest for report writing, I was just making a mess of things anyway. I went to the gym and swam. About half way through my swim, I had to get out of the pool, go to the bathroom and barf up all the Dew I had today. I finished my mile, but lost track of what time I did it in. When I went to my locker to change, I found a message from Ruben on my pager. I called him up and he asked me to meet him and Renado at the usual hole in the wall.

When I got there, the guys were already at our table. My hair was still wet from swimming/showering, and they made jokes about it as if to mask their worry about what was happening. Renado asked me how my training for the Police Olympics was going. Ruben interrupted, "Are you kidding me? That's all she does now. I can't get any work out of her anymore. All she does is run and swim, the little bitch." They both laughed, and I said, "Yea, yea, yea, yuck it up boneheads." Ruben said, "There she goes again. Renado, go and get me some soap out of the bathroom, I'm going to do Ben a favor and wash that little mouth out with soap."

"O.K., enough of having fun at my expense. Spill it Ruben, what happened?" I asked. Ruben explained, "It's that Fucking Weasel Easel!" As Ruben said "Fucking," I kicked him in the shins under the table. Ruben grabbed his leg and yelled, "Owe, what the hell was that for?" I said, "You kiss your wife and kids with that mouth!" Renado laughed. Ruben said, "As I was saying, before I was rudely interrupted, Weasel ratted me out about something that happened six or seven years ago. I had my kids in my G-ride cause I had to drop them off at the sitters. We got a call on a load, and I didn't have a car to take them as mine was in the shop, and I didn't have time to take them, drop them off, and then come back and get my G-ride anyway. I picked Weasel up first, and he saw me do this." Renado said, "That's it? Unbelievable!" I reminded them of how if Easel was just coming forward with this information now, then he should be in trouble too for failure to report Ruben when it happened."

I then told them about what had just happened with Gray transporting a very drunk King and her alcohol in Gray's G-ride. I told them that I was going to report it, and demand that Gray come under the same fire as Ruben. Ruben looked at me with only the corners of his eyes, and a smirk on his face, and said "Yeah right." Renado joined in, "Yeah, they're not going to go after their boy, oh no, ah huh." I responded with, "Yeah, but IA's unwillingness to go after Weasel for not reporting the Ruben/G-ride incident in a timely manner and Gray for the Sherry King drunk episode, demonstrates that IA is engaging in selective enforcement of Customs policies. They are proving us right, that IA is the Goon Squad for Customs corrupt management."

Ruben put on a good front as he continued telling us of his grilling by IA. He told the story almost as though he was reading it from a report, detached and unemotional, but I could see the stress on his face. I knew what this would do to him financially if they gave him the maximum punishment of 45 days off with no pay. Ruben had been through a divorce and had to fight for custody of his kids several times over the past couple of years. With his new wife and baby, combined with this, I knew that this would just about break him financially. As I sat there listening to him, I held in my concern. I wanted to cry, but instead, I made stupid jokes and funny insults. My stomach started burning again, and I felt sick.

That night I told Ben what was going on. He just couldn't believe what was happening to us. He saw how worried I was, and attempted to put me at ease by taking me to the movies to get my mind off of things. After the movies we had a good talk. Ben said, "I can see the stress getting to you Darlene. It's affecting us, it's affecting our sex life, and it is wearing you down. I'm not blaming you, and I think that you are doing the best you can. If it weren't for your workout sessions, I'm sure that you would be biting everyone's head off every day. If this were happening to me, I'd have decked someone by now." I knew that he was right, and I held him tight. I wanted to cry, but I couldn't. I was afraid that if I ever started crying, I wouldn't be able to stop. I couldn't sleep that night. My chest just kept burning, and it felt like an elephant was standing on it. I just kept reliving everything that was happening, over and over in my head again, looking for some kind of magical answer. The only thing that came to mind was what my mom taught me. Drink milk for heartburn. It coats your stomach. I got up and drank some milk.

The next day I reported Gray and King to IA. Our office Investigative Aid Yolanda Rios agreed to be a witness and spoke to the IA agent over the speakerphone with Ruben and me. I was very proud of Yolanda for being honest and having a spine to take this stand with us. We all knew that she would face retaliation for this and her coming forward took a lot of guts.

On February 16, 1999, I got my usual midnight warning phone call from Sector (Customs National Dispatch Center), advising me that I had to be in Thermal, at the airport at 0600 for a load (controlled delivery of narcotics) from Calexico. When I hung up the phone, I was half asleep and wondered if the call was real or if I had just dreamed it again. I remembered how a couple of years ago I dreamed of a load call, got up, did my usual getting ready in 15 minutes, jumped in my car and left. As I was attempting to come up on the radio to ascertain where I was supposed to be, Sector (Customs nation-wide dispatch) seemed confused. After much checking, and a push (agent slang for call) to my boss via the radio, I realized that I had dreamed that I received this call.

The next morning when I walked into the office, Allen Casey came over the intercom, in a radio voice, "Ah Sector, Sector, where am I supposed to be Sector?" "915, 915, (my call sign) you're dreaming 915, click your heals three times and then you can go home." As I walked down the hall in total humiliation, Ruben and Jerry walked past me with their arms up, like they were sleepwalking, giggling. Of course my intelligent response was to attempt not to grin and to mutter "Ass holes" under my breath. Later that morning Bob Mattivi came over the intercom and stated, "Everyone involved in tomorrow's escapades please retire to the back for the briefing; oh, and Earth to Darlene, Earth to Darlene, Darlene, wake up. This is a real message." My follow-up, intelligent response was to get on the intercom and say, "Ah Bob, screw you, screw you." When I walked to the back, everyone was pretending to be asleep and snoring.

Well, unfortunately, this was real. Once again, they were waking everyone up at midnight to give them a heads-up for a load at 0600. I thought to myself, why do they do this? Why don't they just let us sleep until 0400 or 0500 and then wake us up? It is always so hard for me to get back to sleep. Still, it will be nice to see the boys from Calexico. As much as Evantie has tried to undermine relationships between RAIC/RV and Calexico, to make Ricardo look bad, some of us see right through the evil rat.

The load came in late, as usual, at about noon. It was hot in Thermal (115 degrees), and I had little sleep. When the boys from the Calexico office pulled up, Carlos Osorio was with them. Carlos is a great agent, Latino, a member of the ACEC, and my friend. He walked over and gave me a big bear hug. I glanced at Dave Gray, and he had a condescending look on his face. I so wanted to walk over, curl my little fist up, and knock that smirk off of his face. What a bigot, I thought.

The load ended up in a bad part of LA, where they always seem to end up. We had to hook up with the SAIC/LA guys. By this time, Ruben, Carlos and I were looked upon with fear and disgust because of our whistle blowing. The LA guys treated us like they were afraid to be seen talking to us, like we had the plague. Some of these guys I have known for years and had sat with for hours on details, and had gone through some dicey situations with. Now, none of them would make eye contact with me. I concealed the hurt and feeling of betrayal by making my usual bad jokes.

We briefed up, and Carlos, Ruben and I were on the entry team. Oohh, there's a shock. I'm sure the LA guys saw us as expendable. Carlos was first to do the knock and notice, supposedly because of his Spanish skills. Funny how that worked out. We had a uniform LAPD officer with us, who also spoke Spanish, but Carlos was still lead in. I was next and then was Ruben. Out of 13 guys, we three were the entry team. I stood there remembering the "Surviving Armed Confrontation Course" that we had recently completed. I remembered them saying that the most dangerous part of an entry was the second and third position of the entry team. When the first guy enters, often times the crooks haven't the time to react, but the second and third person in are like sitting ducks in the doorway, no matter how fast your moving. I said to Ruben and Carlos, "Is this the big hint or what?" I thought, well, Carlos is so big, I'll just tuck in behind him, hold on to his shirt, and hope for the best.

By this time it was 2000 hours. The crooks took a long time getting from Thermal to LA. I told Ruben, "Don't they know how tired I am. Ruben responded, "I see you got the stupid midnight heads-up call too. Why doesn't someone have sense enough to call us the next morning; why wake us up twice?" I said, "My thoughts exactly." Carlos subtly pulled Ruben and I aside, and quietly said, "Nice entry team they put together here huh. Notice how the case agent can't seem to ascertain whether or not this house has any firearms registered, a real no-brainer for the rest of us. Look, we go in fast and low. I'll go right, Dar left, Ruben straight. Remember, low and fast. I don't like the looks of this at all." I thought well there goes my human barricade.

We went in fast and hard. I went left into the kitchen, and there were two toddlers in highchairs at the table. When I came around the doorway, I entered the room with my gun drawn, and the toddlers screamed. I lowered my gun, and quickly holstered it. I then tried to quiet the toddlers. God, this always makes me feel like shit. I scared these little kids to death, and now I have to calm them down. I noticed that they were in there alone, strapped to their chairs. It seemed as though they had been there for a while. The Cheerios on their highchair tables were stale, and their diapers were smelly and soiled.

Carlos gave the all clear signal. I unstrapped the kids and took them to the living room, holding and comforting them. I gave one of them my badge and the other my keys to play with. I noticed that they both needed changing very badly and that this residence was a total dive. I asked one of the LA guys where the mom was, and he answered, "She's probably one of the crack-heads blown out in here (pointing toward the bedroom) with the others; typical dirt-bag Mexicans." I looked over to the stairwell, and saw Ruben standing at the top of the stairs. Unbeknown to the LA guy, Ruben heard this comment. I saw the pain on his face. When he saw me reading him, he looked embarrassed, turned his head, paused, and walked back up the stairs. I thought of how many times in the past year that I had seen this pain, not only on Ruben, but on my Latin husband as well. Part of me wanted to head-butt the LA agent with a shotgun, and part of me wanted to run after Ruben and console him, but all I did was find some Pampers, change the toddlers, and remind myself that we came through the door alive, and that was something.

This little escapade gave Ruben, Carlos and I a chance to talk. We explained to Carlos more about what we were doing in organizing the ACEC (Association of Customs Employees for Change). Carlos was very supportive, however, even in a big, tough-guy, bruiser like Carlos, I saw fear. When the toughest people around you are afraid, the world can be a pretty insecure place, with nowhere to run and hide.

I got home late that night because the search warrant and suspect booking took forever. I had been up for over 24 hours now. I was just in time to chug some more coffee, have breakfast with my kids, and go back to work. My little Ian said, "Mom, I missed you at breakfast and when I came home from school yesterday." I said, "I missed you too handsome, but I'm here now. Can I eat with you?" Sarah and Ian responded with great big hugs. I was so tired, for a split second I thought of how I could go upstairs and grab a few winks, but I had breakfast with my kids instead. I worried about how this job was affecting my role as a parent, and then I reminded myself of the fact that my kids were never strapped to a highchair for hours with soiled diapers, and stale Cheerios while I smoked crack in the next room. Once again, a weak attempt at making myself feel better about this job.

I arrived at the office about 0900 hours. As I was pulling into the parking lot, Ruben was getting out of his car. Both of us were getting 911 pages from Sandy. Ruben looked at me looking at my pager and said, "You too? That Sandy and her 911 pages. You know I love her to death, but you just never know if it is a real 911, or if it is just some juicy info." I said, "I know. I told her to stop doing that and she just doesn't listen."

Ruben and I did a three-way call to Sandy, and she was crying. She told us that she and Shannon Getz were going to be interviewed today by IA, and it had something to do with Huge World. I instructed her to take a tape recorder in there and a witness. She told me that she didn't have one. I told her stop what she was doing, right now, and go and get one. She assured me that she would. When Ruben and I hung up, I again saw pain on his face. Ruben said, "those jerks, they are never going to stop are they Darlene?" As much as Ruben liked to bitch and moan about how Sandy and I drove him crazy, I knew that Ruben cared deeply about us and what was happening to us. I knew he somehow felt a sense of responsibility for what was happening to us, and it wore on him. I tried a lame attempt at "bucking us both up." "Ruben, Sandy's tuff. When she gets through crying she'll be pissed, and handle this like the pro that she is. She's tuff Ruben, she can handle this." I said. I felt that all too familiar burning sensation at the pit of my stomach. I wasn't sure if it was the 7 gallons of coffee and Mountain Dew I had drunk in the past 30 hours, or if it was the rage of all of this that was burning a hole through me.

Sandy called me later that day, and gave me the low down. She sounded much better. She sounded like the brave fighter I knew her to be, and I was relieved. She had gotten a recorder and recorded the session. Sure enough, IA was grilling her about Huge World. Huge World was a technology network-marketing group that Sandy, Ervin Rios, and I had all joined. For a nominal entry fee, you become a distributor, and get technology products at a reduced rate. It kind of worked like Avon, but for technology. I was interested in the Internet course they offered. None of us had any intention of selling any of these products; we only wanted to get the products and training that was offered at some really decent rates.

I couldn't believe that this is what IA was going to hang their hat on. I briefed Ruben over lunch (more Mountain Dew to stay awake), and used the phrase rat-bastards frequently. At 1500 hrs, I had been awake for 36 hours straight. I drank so much Mountain Dew that my hands were shaking. I thought to myself, Mt. Dew should do a commercial with Federal Narcotics Agents on how we all use it to stay awake on the job. I wasn't sure if I was shaking from the Dew, the rage of what happened to Sandy, or the lack of sleep. It was probably a combination of them all. I went to the gym, and with every stroke I imagined myself placing my hands around Drake Brinkley's neck, and strangling him with my bare hands. I swam the mile in 52 minutes. I'll have to try getting livid and drinking a ton of the Dew for the police Olympics.

On March 10, 1999, SA Janet Somers informed Ruben that Easel had admitted to her as well as SA Scott Chandler, of the SAIC/LA office and AUSA Bailey Miller in September 1998, that Easel did in fact take the heroin home. This would be instrumental in our proof that there is selective enforcement of regulations on agents and that enforcement of agency policy is used only on whistleblowers, not the "good old boys." Ruben contacted me at the U.S. Attorney's office to tell me this news. I was there picking up subpoenas, one of which I would have to serve in Calexico. I told Ruben that he needed to go with me to serve this subpoena, and that this would give us a perfect opportunity to brief Ricardo Sandoval, the RAIC (Resident Agent In Charge)/Calexico about the upcoming ACEC (Association of Customs Employees for Change) meeting.

Chapter 19

Trip to Calexico

When I got back to the office I signed out for the next day with Ruben, to Calexico to serve subpoenas. Now in the federal agent world, serving subpoenas is a routine, normal course of business, type of thing. We simply sign out where we are going to be, and no one ever asks any questions. As soon as Evantie saw that Ruben and I were going to go to Calexico, he acted out of character. He came into my office and approached me at my desk. He asked, "Ah, hey Dar, what's this you're going to Calexico for?" I showed him the subpoena. He looked at me with a stumped look on his face and said, "So you have to go to Calexico then; or can't you just mail this or something?" I thought to myself, what a dunce. Where did he get his training from, Wal-Mart School of Investigators? Everyone knows (anyone that has ever completed a successful criminal case that is) that these federal criminal subpoenas have to be served in person. I responded in a suspicious tone of voice, "Yes boss, it has been a standing requirement from the U.S. Attorney's office for years now that these have to be delivered in person." Evantie said, "Oh, O.K., just wondering what was going on."

Evantie went back to his office, and in less than one minute later, he returned. I was on the phone, and he stood there looking at me impatiently, and you could feel the worry/anxiety oozing from his every being. I was concluding my conversation, and Evantie was visibly pissed off because I didn't immediately hang up on the caller and jump to attention. Evantie sighed and made a twirling finger gesture to me, indicting that I needed to hang up and give him immediate attention.

As I watched him twirl his finger at me with his condescending look, I fantasized about grabbing his finger, placing it in my large stapler, and driving a staple through it. What a Dick this guy was!

I hung up the phone and said, "What do you need boss?" Evantie asked, "Why do you need to take Ruben with you?" Again I thought, what a stupid clown. I said in a condescending tone of voice, "Evantie, It's standard agency policy that no agent will serve a subpoena alone, regarding officer safety." Evantie replied, "I know that, but why are you taking Ruben?" I answered his obviously paranoid question with a question, "Why not Ruben? I mean is there some kind of problem here sir? Are agents now being told whom they can or can't take with them to serve a subpoena? I mean, I've worked here 11 years now, and no one has ever questioned me, or anyone else, as to the selection of agents to serve subpoenas." I knew what Evantie was up to. He was going to try to keep Ruben and me from having contact with Ricardo Sandoval. He knew we would make good use of our time, and this just killed him. Evantie, stumbling for a stupid answer said, "Well I was just concerned as to whether Ruben was available or not." I said, "Sir, I wouldn't have put him on the sign out board if I hadn't already cleared it with him."

As he stood there trying to cleverly disguise his agenda with a bad acting job of concern, and desperately trying to come up with his next genius idea of why Ruben and I couldn't go to Calexico, I got pissed off. I looked at him, shook my head in disgust, reached for the phone, started dialing, and said, "You know what Evantie, why don't I call the AUSA Yvette and let you explain all these concerns of yours to her of how you don't want me to do my job on this case. I'd really like to hear your explanation to a federal prosecutor of why her subpoena isn't going to be served." Evantie said in a spineless tone of voice, "No, no, that's all right, I just don't understand why you have to take Ruben with you." I shot back, " And you still haven't given me justification as to why not Ruben!" Evantie sighed in exasperation and walked away. As he walked away I flipped him off, and fantasized about throwing the stapler through his head.

On March 11, 1999, Ruben came to my house to pick me up for our trip to Calexico. Our original game plan was to ride together, and leave one vehicle at my house. After Ruben arrived, we thought it better to drive both vehicles to the I-10 frwy split at the Beaumont exit. We'd then leave one vehicle there, and carpool to Calexico. This would save Ruben a drive back to my house at the end of the day. Ruben lived north of the I-10 Frwy, in Oak Glen, and I lived South of the I-10 frwy in Hemet (aprox. 45 minute commute for Ruben). Ruben walked out of my house first to go to his vehicle. I got in the doorway, and went back in to turn my T.V. off. Ruben had already made it to his car, turned around and headed up the street as I was approaching my car. As I walked to my car door, I observed an obvious surveillance vehicle watching us. The vehicle started down the street straight towards my house and the driver, upon spotting me, ducked into a parking space. It was real obvious that the driver of this car seemed startled to see me about to get into my car. I stopped my entrance into my car, turned towards this strange car (never saw this car in my neighborhood before), and stared at it. The driver pulled a fast U-turn, and sped off.

As if this bonehead maneuver wasn't obvious enough, when I got into my car and started to catch up with Ruben, there was another strange vehicle parked on the next block. As I drove past it I slowed way down, and maneuvered my vehicle over to the drivers side (opposite side of the street) of the parked, strange vehicle. There was someone attempting to duck down on the driver's side, hiding. I then heard several long squelch sounds come over my radio. I had learned from several sources, one of which was Mr. IA himself, David Gray, that when IA is conducting a surveillance on their secret stealth channel their radio transmissions come over our radios as squelch. I wanted to alert Ruben on the radio, but I knew that the IA stealth rocket scientists would be listening. I floored it to catch up with Ruben. I caught up with him a few blocks away, and lit him up (turned my police lights on). He saw me, and stayed at the light. I jumped out of my car, ran up to him at the intersection, and quickly explained what I had just seen.

We drove to the I-10 frwy, and parked my car in the Denny's parking lot. I jumped in with Ruben, and we began to conduct counter-surveillance to lose our tail. Ruben explained that I had probably startled them when they first came around the corner and saw me at my car. I wasn't supposed to be there. They obviously thought that I would be leaving with Ruben from my house, in his car. The morons didn't count on us leaving in separate vehicles. When they saw Ruben leave, they obviously thought that I was with him, and they were trying to catch up to us in Ruben's vehicle when I came out of my house.

We saw several more obvious bonehead stunts, and burned (slang term for identifying a surveillance) the IA surveillance to the ground. Ruben, being the clever, street savvy agent that he was, lost the IA stooges lickity-split. Ruben and I couldn't believe how stupid and obvious these morons were. I was convinced that before Customs issued their IA decoder ring, they gave each IA agent a frontal lobotomy.

It took us about three hours to get to Calexico. When we got there, Ricardo was very happy to see us. He greeted us with warmth and professional hospitality. His office was unlike any government supervisor's office I'd ever seen. He had a beautiful portrait of Dr. Martin Luther King, and the Mexican flag hanging in his office. His office didn't have the normal narcissistic cop memorabilia hanging all over. It looked very classy and professional. We talked for a while, and then he invited us to lunch. As we walked to his car, a vehicle passed us in the parking lot. Ricardo told us that it was an IA vehicle, that he'd seen it all too many times. We sat in his vehicle for a while talking, and that same vehicle passed us, circling in the parking lot, at least three time. Ricardo said, "Can you believe this shit. These morons have nothing better to do but to nose around us." We told him about how we were surveilled from the house, and he was not surprised. Ricardo said laughingly, "Welcome to the club guys. Now you know what my life has been like for a couple of years now. They follow me to work, they follow me home. My life is no longer my own; I have no privacy." As he spoke I could feel the pain and anguish in his voice. His face was a road map of suffering as his tired eyes watched the IA puke pass by us again.

We drove to a nearby restaurant, and sat in a booth by the window. We could see the IA vehicle had followed us there, and passed by several times. Ricardo explained in great detail of how when he became a whistleblower several years ago and filed his lawsuit, how his life was literally ripped from his grasp. He told us one story after another of the consistent and ongoing retaliation he had received at the hands of Internal Affairs. The fact that he used to be one of them (an IA investigator) mattered not. He became under one bogus IA investigation after another, always being cleared at the end. He was currently under the 22nd bogus investigation. I listened as he told us of how this had almost destroyed his family life, and of how he too had started using working out as a tool to relieve stress. Everyday after work he would go to the gym and lift weights. As he spoke, I noticed how buffed he was, and thought of just how many hours and how much work it must have taken to get to that state. Then I thought of myself, of how I was running and swimming myself to death just to keep from strangling Evantie or Brinkley. As I listened to him I also watched Ruben's face reflect the same pain and anguish. I wanted to cry, but I knew that if I ever started crying, I'd never be able to stop. My heart ached for Ricardo's tragic story, and my rage began to burn a hole through my stomach. I ordered a tall glass of milk with my lunch.

One of the stories that Ricardo told that I found most appalling, was the one about the "Mexican Parking Lot." Before Brinkley became the Director for the Office of Investigations, he was the ASAIC (Assistant Special Agent In Charge)/San Diego. Brinkley and several other managers had what they called "The Mexican Parking Lot." This was where all Latinos had to park their old, beaten up G-rides (slang for government assigned vehicle). No Latinos were ever issued good cars, and Brinkley made them park in a lot away from the office, so as not to embarrass the image of the SAIC office. Ricardo worked at the SAIC/San Diego at the time, and was treated like this. I explained to Ricardo how this was exactly what was currently happening to Ruben at our RAIC office.

As I listened to this, it sickened me. My hatred for Brinkley, and others like him grew dark and deep. I couldn't help but think of all the times my poor husband (also Latino) tried to point out obvious discrimination to me, and I just didn't see it. I would always tell him that he was just seeing things; that he was paranoid. How I wished I could take those words back, and wished that I had listened to him and offered some support, and consolation. White chick or not, I would never see things through white Anglo eyes again. I would never distrust my husband's judgment again.

As I drove home from the Denny's that night, I felt that every car was watching me. I felt like I had been stripped naked in a crowd of strangers. I felt paranoid, violated, frustrated, and angry. I thought of how this must have worn on Ricardo to feel like this every day of his life for over two years. No amount of money from a lawsuit, or no promotion could ever make up for this. These lowlifes took this man's life away, and I saw first hand what that did to him. I don't know how he's kept it together for so long. I hadn't endured half of the bullshit he had received, and already it was all I could do to keep from running over Evantie and Brinkley in a parking lot. I worried that I wouldn't have the courage or stamina to go the distance like Ricardo has. My mind raced with anguish, fear and rage. I almost had a wreck on the freeway, for inattentive driving.

On March 29, 1999, I certified mailed an affidavit and formal complaint to the Director of the Regional EEO Complaint Center regarding the role SAIC/Los Angeles and RAIC/Riverside management played in the refusal of the Postal Inspectors to even lift a finger to investigate the crimes committed against me (i.e. the threatening letter, and phony transcript). On April 2, 1999, I received at my home a response from the Regional Complaint Center, regarding these very same issues. This response had a date stamped March 30, 1999, and signed by Luanne Holmes, Director. In this response Ms. Holmes dismisses my formal complaint stating that it is not within the purview of the EEO regulations. Now, the $64 question is, how in the hell can my formal complaint be dismissed on March 30th, when my formal complaint was only received at the Regional Complaint Center on April 1, 1999 (date verified via certified mail return receipt)?????? I subsequently wrote a letter to Ms. Holmes with copies of the certified mail returned receipt. I asked Ms. Holmes where it was that she obtained her ESP abilities that she could know the contents of a complaint, and turn it down before she even read it. I got no response.

Chapter 20

ACEC

On April 5, 1999, I attended a meeting of the Association of Customs Employees for Change (ACEC) at the Mission Inn, Riverside, California. Sandy Nunn, Ruben Sandoval, Rick Sandoval, Marissa New, and Justine Pierce who was the second in command for EEO at the Customs headquarters level were present. The purpose of the meeting was to establish a united front and an organization (ACEC) to fight the cronyism and corruption that we had all encountered. We presented plenty of evidence that would more than prove our point to Justin Pierce. Pierce subsequently ensured us that he would be a facilitator between the Customs Commissioner and us. Ruben wanted to trust him, but I was still very leery. I told Ruben that it didn't matter if this guy was honorable or not, if he pushed the wrong buttons, and didn't actively participate in shutting us down, Pierce would just become one of us; the Commissioner would simply kill his own messenger (figuratively speaking).

At this meeting I read a letter to the whole group, out loud. Sandy Nunn authored this letter. It was an excellent, professional, yet, scathing letter reporting much of the corruption, cronyism, and retaliation that we had witnessed. With Sandy, the pen really is mightier than the sword. This letter had a petition style of attachment that contained the signatures of 26 Customs employees (including inspectors, agents, supervisors, intelligence analyst etc). This letter was sent the day prior to this meeting, to numerous Senators and Congressmen particularly in our state of California, as well as Customs Commissioner Ray Kelly and

Customs Commissioner of Internal Affairs Harrison Wells. As I read the letter aloud, I could see Pierce squirming in his chair. He was not pleased, but I clearly was. He gave me a look as if to say, "You go too far." I glared back at him intensely as I read, as if to say, "I've only just begun." As I read the letter aloud, every emotion that I'd been feeling was aching to come to the surface. I gritted my teeth and chocked down my rage, and anguish. My face felt hot and I thought I was going to have a stroke trying to maintain control and dignity. When I finished, I looked upon the faces of everyone in that room and could see the same road map of emotional grind. I then looked at Justine Pierce who was also observing the emotion of the room, and on his face I saw fear and hopelessness. I then knew that not only wouldn't he help us, but also even if he wanted to he knew it was futile. My rage evolved into hope-lessness and I stood quiet for the remainder of the meeting.

During a break in this meeting, Ricardo Sandoval gave me a copy of a statement by Robert Saitley. Robert Saitley was an ASAIC (Assistant Special Agent In Charge) under SAIC (Special Agent In Charge)/Los Angeles Drake Brinkley. Saitley had been running the largest under-cover money laundering operation ever conducted by any agency in U.S. history, Operation Casablanca. Saitley read a statement before the House of Representatives Subcommittee on Criminal Justice, Drug Policy and Human Resources. The following are excerpts from this statement:

> "Beginning in the fall of 1997, Mr. Drake Brinkley leaked information about Operation Casablanca. At a law enforcement conference in Tampa, Florida, Mr. Brinkley provided information about this undercover operation to a network news executive.
>
> Later in the investigation, Mr. Brinkley invited sev-eral congressional staff representatives to Los Angeles to be briefed on a major undercover money laundering

investigation. Upon their arrival he not only paraded them through the undercover offsite, which housed the Alpha Task Force, he took them to the audio and video monitoring station of the undercover storefront, "Golden Empire."

On page seven of this statement Mr. Saitley states: "During my meeting with the Commissioner of Customs, I requested an official document which reports the findings of the Internal Affairs investigation related Mr. Brinkley's false and malicious accusation. To this day, I have received no official response from any Customs Service Officer in regard to any of the topics I discussed with the Commissioner."

As I read Robert Saitly's statement I thought, "poor bastard." Now Saitly is going to have the IA goon squad after him just like the rest of us whistleblowers. I didn't know Saitly that well, but the general consensus was that he was an honorable and direct man, and an excellent manager. I was familiar with some of his casework, and I found him to be impressive, and professional. Saitly had definitely "been there, done that" which is more that anyone could ever say about Brinkley. I remarked to Ricardo about what a crock of shit this is. Here I got a letter of disciplinary action for allegedly releasing confidential information in submitting letters of commendation to EEO, but Brinkley exposes an undercover investigation and two undercover sites endangering the lives of undercover agents and confidential sources, and walks away clean.

Where's IA when it comes to the Customs MAFIA managers? I further stated to Ricardo that, "You just watch; now magically Robert Saitly will come under some sort of bogus IA investigation." Ricardo responded, "He already has Dar. He already has." Just then it hit me. Operation Casablanca was targeting the infamous Arellano-Felix narcotics smuggling cartel. My tanker car seizure, and subsequent investigation was targeting the same organization. I had information verifying that the dope I seized was in fact Arellano-Felix dope. My head started spinning. Here Brinkley had made it his personal vendetta to undermine not only my criminal case, but he torpedoed the entire rail project as well. Simultaneously, Brinkley was torpedoing Saitly's bazillion dollar undercover money laundering projects. As I put two and two together a rush of adrenalin hit me like a brick on the head.

As soon as the ACEC meeting was over, I told Ruben I had to split. He and the others wanted me to stay and strategize some more, and I told them I had to get back to the office. Ruben sensed that something was up and asked, "Wow Dar, what's going on?" I looked at him and said, "I'm not sure yet, but I feel that this house of cards may be a cumin down." I went back to the office and plowed into the Customs automated systems of importations. I began pulling entries of cars that I had looked at. At the beginning of my rail project, I had put what's called a "General Hold" on all pressurized tanker cars coming into the U.S., for weight. This meant that no car should have been cleared by any Customs officer without the car first being directed to one of the only two rail yards that can do this (Texas and Colton California). I immediately found several releases that were not authorized. I wasn't as familiar with this portion of the Customs computer system. This system was mostly designed for inspectors, so I immediately got a hold of Ervin Rios and asked to meet him.

Chapter 21

The Pieces Fit

Ervin was about to pull his shift at UPS. We agreed to meet at his office. When I walked in he knew something was up. I asked him, "Who has the authority to release a general hold placed by O.I. (Customs term for Office of Investigations the Agents chain of command / I&C was the acronym for Customs Inspection and Control the Inspectors chain of command). Ervin answered, "Only a supervisor, with subsequent notification to the agent." I said, "Ervin, are you sure about that?" Ervin leaned toward me with a mountain of curiosity and said, "Why Dar, what's going on? What do you got?" I took the entries from inside the jacket I was wearing and just as I was going to show them to him, his supervisor walked in. I quickly concealed them back in my jacket, as stealthy as I could. I felt my heart pounding, and my head racing. We made small talk with the supervisor, told him some lame cover story of what I was doing there, and then he left.

I pulled out the entries, and showed him what I had found. He explained to me that there was a space on the entry where the supervisor releasing the general hold, by regulation, was supposed to put in his four-digit code. I remembered of how on the last three tanker cars we were trying to look at, they had been released three times, and I had to get the railroad to chase them down three times, and send them back from central California to be weighed. Ervin pulled up the car numbers (every rail car has a distinct 8 or 9 digit code for tracking, identification, and billing/invoicing purposes). Sure enough, Customs personnel, not a blunder by the railroad as I had previously thought, had also released these cars. I showed Ervin the statement of Robert Saitly, and he quickly put two and two together. Ervin's eyes got big, and he started to breath hard.

Ervin went to his desk, and unlocked a drawer. He pulled out a file that he had been keeping under lock and key. As he pulled the file out, he looked out the glass window to make sure no one was coming. He showed me this hand written flow chart he had done. It all stemmed from a seizure of cocaine he had made at the airport from this juvenile, and a private jet that he cleared from a Colombian private airline. Ervin's flow chart tracked the Arellano-Felix Cartel to two private aircraft that were conveniently owned by Mexican and Columbian banks. These banks were profiled in Robert Saitly's Casablanca Investigation/undercover money laundering operation. Ervin further tracked the Pilot of the aircraft where he seized the cocaine from the juvenile, to a company in Sineloa, Mexico. The name of this company was Grassa; the same name on the entry documents for the tanker car-load of Arellano-Felix dope that I seized almost one year ago. Ervin said, "You know Dar, when I seized the coke from this kid, my supervisor was all over me. He acted extremely pissed off, and tried to undermine me, all at the direction of the Port Director, Wyndal Nabrowski."

Then Ervin said, "There's more. There's an ex-inspector who I have spoken with, his name is Jeff Weitzman." When Ervin said this name, it rang a bell with me. Ervin continued, "His name rings a bell because he was the inspector who nailed the famous "Hydro" rail tanker load of cocaine at the Otay Mesa port of entry." I said, "Oh yea, I remember." Ervin said, "Well when Weitzman profiled this car, he put a hold on it in ACS for secondary (the location that inspectors move vehicles to for inspection/entry). Someone released the hold without authorization, and it was a coincidence that Weitzman was working the line and just happened to see it coming. Weitzman secondaried it anyway, and just as he was about to run his dog on it, his supervisor ordered him to release it. Weitzman ran the dog any way, and the dog went crazy. Weitzman defied the orders of his supervisor, and popped it open to find one of the biggest seizures of cocaine ever. When Weitzman confronted his supervisor about who ordered the car released, the supervisor said it was by order of the Port Director, Adrian Garcia."

I sat back in my chair and shook my head. It was commonly known throughout the agency that Adrian Garcia had been under one corruption investigation after another by the FBI. He was infamous for being rumored to be in bed with the Arellano-Felix Cartel. Ervin then pulled out a picture from his file. It was a picture of Adrian Garcia with his Customs uniform on, with his arm around Carlos Ray Horn, infamous leader of a Mexican smuggling cartel that works with the Arellano-Felix Organization. I said, "Holy cow! Ervin, did you know that Adrian Garcia and Brinkley go way back?" Ervin said that he had heard that, but wasn't sure. I added that I had also heard that Ervin's prior Port Director, Wyndal Nabrowski, was a big buddy with both Garcia and Drake Brinkley. These people all came up together within Customs. Brinkley had worked the southern border on and off for approximately 30 years.

Then Ervin rolled his chair even closer to me, and in almost a whisper he said, "Dar, do you remember back in the late 1980's—through the early 1990's hearing about the "Blue Ribbon Commission Investigation" initiated by Congress?" I responded, "Yeah, as a matter of fact I remember it very well. At that time, I was assigned to the Commissioner of Customs Personal Protection Detail, every time she came to L.A. She spoke quite often of this investigation, and having to respond to Congress." Ervin said, "Well, I have the entire two thousand-and-something page transcript of those proceedings; and you know what, the same assholes that we're dealing with, Brinkley, Nabrowski, and Mr. IA himself, Harrison Wells, all their names are all over that investigation. There was a female OIG investigator named Cherry Rollins, and an attorney/private investigator by the name of Jason Fielding assigned to the Congressional Investigation. Cherry Rollins resigned from the OIG in disgust because of all of the stonewalling that she received from Customs in her efforts to conduct her investigation. Jason Fielding was found in his driveway in Long Beach, two to the chest, and one to the head. It was ruled a botched burglary attempt—I'm not buying it. Who else shoots like that? Only cops. This poor bastard was executed in his driveway in front of his little daughter. No doubt he stumbled onto something just like we did."

Ervin then stated, "Dar, think of the timing of when I got fired. Think of what we were doing." Just then it hit me, and I said, "Oh my god; that was right after we did the first tanker car, and we started working in the rail yard." Ervin said, "That's right! My supervisor was giving me hell every step of the way; he didn't want me working on the rail project with you at all. Darlene, this isn't a coincidence! They don't want us working these rail cars for a reason. We're not supposed to be over there! And doesn't it kind of make you wonder about your "Geraldo Rivera" tanker car? Maybe it wasn't so empty after all!"

My mind started racing. I began to recall about how we were all so sure that there was no way that anyone could have unloaded that tanker car during the trip up from Calexico and the time frame that it was unaccounted for. At the time, we were all so sure that the only way that they could have opened that car and removed the contents was via a specialized facility, like the one in Colton. The commodity contained in the car at that time was some sort of fuel. Then I thought of how easy it was for the crooks on this last loaded car to simply "jerry rig" a tri-pod on top of the hatch, and use a simple pulley and chain device hooked up to two fork lifts; poof the hatch was opened. What we had originally thought to be almost impossible became the practical. The lost "Geraldo Rivera" car was unaccounted for approximately 9 to 12 hours. This would have been time for the crooks to track this car off onto a small spur, somewhere between Calexico and Colton, and then access the load. Based upon what happened to this last loaded car on the controlled delivery, this wasn't out of the realm of possibilities anymore. In fact, when you're talking about the kind of money we're dealing with (millions of dollars in narcotics), it is well within the realm of possibilities. As I thought of this, I sat back in my chair in total disillusion, feeling like a fool who had just realized just how bad I'd been had. I recalled how there I was, defending my agency to the media. The media had been making the accusation that the tanker empty car (Geraldo Rivera car) was in fact loaded, and that during the time frame that it was unaccounted for, the crooks off-loaded it.

Had they been right? Had I foolishly assumed the best of my agency, and failed to dig into these accusations because of my naive loyalty to my agency and inexperience at the time? Ervin saw me sitting there in a blank stare, and waved his hand back and forth in front of my face as he was saying, "Earth to Darlene, Earth to Darlene, come in please." He got my attention and said, "Dar, I'm thinking that you're thinking that the "Geraldo Rivera" car was loaded, and the crooks got to the stuff just like they did this last one, with a tri-pod and everything. That is what you're thinking isn't it?" I looked at him with an "oh no, I screwed up" look on my face, and shook my head yes. Ervin said, "Dar, if we're right and they killed that private investigator Jason because he found something, just imagine what they would do to cover up the kind of stuff we've found. Maybe he found out the same things. If they've killed once it won't bother them to kill again. I mean, look what they've already done, and they don't even know what we've discovered about this rail car stuff. Think about it Dar, if we're right, this is a billion dollar business we're attempting to disrupt, and people have been killed for a whole lot less."

We both sat there in disbelief. I asked Ervin, "Who else have you shown this stuff to?" Ervin said, "No one." I responded, "Good. Don't." I picked up the phone, and called my AUSA Yvette. I told her that Ervin and I had to meet with her, and couldn't discuss why over the phone. She agreed. When I got off of the phone, Ervin and I looked at each other and began to laugh nervously. I told Ervin, "Dude, I hope this place isn't bugged, or we're toast. Look, do you have any contacts at

LAPD that we could pull the files on this Jason Fielding murder investigation?" Ervin responded with a confident smile, "You know me Dar, I have contacts everywhere." When I left there, for the first time I was riddled with fear, and my rage had taken a back seat. I thought of that poor private investigator being executed in front of his little girl. I was convinced that this wasn't just a robbery. He had found out something he wasn't supposed to know, just like us. I thought of my kids, and my husband, and worried, worried, worried. I was now convinced that my dream really was some sort of warning. These must be some sort of guardian angels sent to give me a message, and the message was coming through loud and clear, "GET OUT!"

On April 21, 1999, I got a call from Sandy Nunn. She told me that Robert Saitley just walked into the SAIC/Los Angeles office, turned in his badge and gun, and retired, before his minimum mandatory retirement. I couldn't believe it. Saitley was one of the toughest men in Customs, and he just threw in the towel and walked away. I began to seriously consider my options, and began to listen to my head, not my ego.

Later that day, Ricardo Sandoval called me. He told me about a girl that used to work for him in IA, and was a good friend of his. This girl, Cynthia Stone, her husband was a DEA agent. About a year or so ago, Cynthia had to attend some IA training at FLETC (Federal Law Enforcement Training Center) with Dave Gray. This was while Gray was still in IA, before he came to the RAIC/Riverside office. Ricardo said that she wanted to talk to me about something, and that he'd call me at home tonight; he didn't trust these phones. Later that night I got a call from Ricardo at home. He told me that while Cynthia Stone and David Gray were at the school, they went to the queer bar (cop slang for the small bar located just outside the gates of FLETC) together one night. Cynthia had a few too many drinks, and Gray acted like a gentleman and offered to walk her back to her dorm. When they got to her dorm, Gray attempted to force himself on her.

Rick said it was all she could do to beat him off. She screamed as loud as she could, he got scared, and left.

The next day, Sandy and I called Cynthia Stone. She told us that the reason she didn't come forward soon after it happened was that she was afraid of Gray and the power he had with IA. She already knew full well how IA was used in this agency. Now she no longer worked for Customs and she was willing to come forward. I assured her that I would relay this information to the appropriate agency. When I got off of the phone with Cynthia and Sandy, I thought to myself, what am I, the whistle blower hotline? I knew that Gray already resented the hell out of me, and well now he's going to hate me. I documented this and Ruben and I reported it to both the Treasury Inspector General's Office, and The FBI.

April 23rd 1999, Ervin Rios and I met with AUSA Yvette Palazuelos. Before we went into her office, Ervin met me outside, and explained to me of how the homicide investigation files of Jason Fielding had magically disappeared, and that his contacts at LAPD were at a loss as to why they couldn't find them. Then he reminded me that our beloved Port Director, Wyndal Nabrowski, used to work for LAPD, and often bragged about all of his contacts there. Ervin said repeatedly, "This is no coincidence Dar, this is no coincidence. These files aren't misplaced or lost, these files are buried!" Additionally, Ervin told me of how several Inspector friends of his had told him that Senator Fienstein was seen a couple of days ago on the Customs Yacht with Drake Brinkley. This was just a few weeks after Sandy's letter (the letter signed by Customs employees alleging corruption) was sent to senators and congressmen, including Senator Fienstein, via certified mail. All of the pieces were coming together like some dark, abstract, unbelievable jigsaw puzzle. I wondered, just how far up does this go? My fear grew.

We went into Yvette's office and explained to her what we had put together, and I showed her the tanker car entry's that had been released. We also showed her the picture of the Customs Port Director with

Cartel leader Carlos Ray Horn, and their long-standing relationship with Drake Brinkley and Harrison Wells. We explained the connections between the Casablanca Money Laundering Operation, and the tanker car case, and of how they both involved the Arellano-Felix Cartel. We further explained our suspicions about Brinkley, Harrison Wells, and the rest, and how it was no coincidence that Brinkley was torpedoing Casablanca as well as the rail project. We also told her about the Congressional Blue Ribbon Commission Investigation into Corruption in Customs some 10 years ago, involving some of the same people, and of the murder of Jason Fielding, the private investigator/attorney who was conducting an investigation into the same people. We told her that we were confident that all of this is not just some coincidence. She listened carefully, seemed very concerned, and told us that she would brief the AUSA's on the Casablanca case.

Chapter 22

The Demonstration

A couple of nights later, Sandy called me up and we discussed the Idea of a demonstration. She got the idea because of the demonstrations that were on going in downtown Riverside, against the Riverside Police. The demonstrators believed that the execution style killing of a black girl who had been asleep in her vehicle was racially motivated. As I thought about this I realized just how much I had changed. Five years ago, I would have immediately defended the cops, and wouldn't have questioned their actions. Now I see these incidents with different eyes, questioning if the cops engaged in police brutality. I clearly remembered the first time that I saw the videotape of the Rodney King beating. I saw with my own two eyes law enforcement at it's worse. I clearly saw cops out of control. Yet the next day when I went to work, all the talk in the office was of explaining how the cops had to react that way. That it was in their training. I remember thinking; I never had training like that. Everyone was immediately coming to the defense of the cops. I thought to myself, well maybe I missed something, or they saw something else that I didn't. This was one topic that, during that time, I stayed clear of. I felt uncomfortable about the whole situation. Maybe because I knew in my heart that what I saw was cops really out of control, and I didn't have the spine to stand up for my opinion of what I know I saw. I would later realize that to be silent about these things is in essence, to be condoning them. Through my silence, I was in fact condoning this type of racist, criminal behavior. I regretted my silence.

Although Sandy's idea scared me and seemed a bit drastic, I started thinking about something someone had recently told me (regarding going public about the suspected corruption in the tanker car case). It was a reporter who was trying to get me to go public, she said, "Sometimes the best protection you can get is when you come into the light." I also thought of the regret I felt about not voicing my opinion regarding the Rodney King incident. I didn't want to be a coward again, and live with the regret. Besides, nothing else had worked for us thus far, so I thought, what the hell. This just might work.

We got our Attorney Tom Allison on the phone (3 way calling) and discussed the idea of a demonstration. Tom added that he had just learned that The Customs Commissioner was scheduled to appear the following Monday in front of a Congressional Committee, and announce how he has everything in Customs well in hand. Tom said, "talk about timing, picture it: here he is bragging to congress about how he has it under control, and then someone interrupts him and tells him that there are Customs Agents demonstrating in front of the RAIC/Riverside, and announcing a huge class action lawsuit for discrimination and retaliation against whistle blowers."

I expressed some concerns about trying to put a demonstration together in such short notice. Sandy assured me that we could do it, so we pushed a call to Ruben. Much to my surprise, Ruben also thought it was a great idea. I was worried about how my husband might react to us going public, so I asked Ruben to talk to him, and he did. Ben was very supportive, but made it clear that he didn't want us discussing the tanker car corruption case. Ruben agreed that it was neither the time nor the place to expose our suspicions; that we should only expose the retaliation against whistle blowers and the class action lawsuit.

After only a couple of days of burning up the phones, and dealing with a logistical nightmare, we put a nice little demonstration together. We were treading on a fine line of trying to keep this somewhat hush-hush (we didn't want management to find out and attempt to stop us) and telling enough people to get them to attend. I anointed Sandy Nunn as the Networking Queen of the Universe. We talked to Cathy Harris, the Atlanta Whistle Blower, and Author of "Flying while Black: A Whistleblower's Story." Harris is a Senior Customs Inspector who blew the whistle on Customs policy of racial profiling black women at the airports. Harris received the same retaliatory treatment as have the rest of us, and was still showing the courage to fly in for the demonstration.

The Friday before the demonstration, both Ruben and I put in for annual leave for the following Monday. We were giggling like two school kids up to no good, as we filled out the leave sheets. I remember a sense of empowerment about what we were doing. I felt brave and confident. How naive of us both.

Several people flew in over the weekend, and Ruben, Tom Allison, and I had a meeting at the Mission Inn Hotel. There we signed the paperwork to incorporate the ACEC, and worked on our speeches. Monday morning all the key players met for breakfast at the Mission Inn. I got to finally meet, in flesh and blood, the people that I had been talking to on the phone for the past year or so; Mike Connor, Cathy Harris, Tom Allison, John Carman, and Stephen Young from Arizona. Tom gave each of us a copy of the press release he had prepared, and it read as follows:

Today, the Association of Customs Employees (ACEC) and the Customs Employees Against Discrimination Association (CEADA) announce their joining of forces to seek a fundamental and important change in how the U.S. Customs Service treats its employees. Tomorrow, the United States Senate will hold hearings on serious problems with the Customs Office of Internal Affairs. Some of these problems have come to light through the efforts of David Kidwell, a reporter for the Miami Herald, and present or former Customs employees who have suffered the denigration of the integrity of the Customs Service.

For too long, the Customs Office of Internal Affairs has been used by unscrupulous management officials to shield themselves and their associates from serious charges of wrongdoing. At the same time these same Customs officials have used Internal Affairs as a sword against those employees who dare challenge their misuse of authority. When employees raise legitimate concerns about management wrongdoing they are often ignored or subjected to retaliation. Employees who dare to file grievances, report wrongdoing, or claim discrimination are perceived to be disloyal to the agency, and thereafter wrongfully targeted for retaliation.

One of the most effective means available to retaliate against employees is the instigation of an Internal Affairs or administrative investigation against an employee. Internal Affairs and/or administrative investigations are undertaken against these employees for what are often petty, frivolous and false charges of wrongdoing. Subjecting Customs employees to unjustified investigation can, and does, ruin the careers of these employees. Unjustified investigation causes them and their families to suffer greatly.

How could these problems fester to the point that the public, many responsible government officials, including the Senate's Finance Committee, the Commissioner of Customs, and Customs employees themselves doubt the integrity of the Service? Because Internal Affairs, hiding under regulations and policies meant to protect legitimate investigations, is allowed to use the same regulations and policies to cover up their blunders and illegal actions. Customs' management reluctance to lift the veil of secrecy has led to the failure of the public trust. So long as the wrongdoers are able to escape public scrutiny for their actions, there will be abuses.

Today, the ACEC and CEADA call for an end to the discriminatory and retaliatory practices of the Customs Service, and those who have, and continue to use the Office of Internal Affairs to discriminate and retaliate against Customs employees. ACEC takes notice of, and hope from, the Commissioner of Customs' recent statement acknowledging the past abuses of Internal Affairs. However, we are here today to voice that retaliatory actions are still being undertaken against good and honest employees, and that the Commissioner's efforts to date have been unsuccessful. Unfortunately, the only means available to those who have been wronged is to band together and bring legal action against Customs. ACEC has therefore retained the Washington, D.C. law firm of Davis & Bentzen, P.L.L.C. to seek legal redress on behalf of its members. The firm may be contacted at (202)000-0000.

Tom's press release was elegant, dignified, and perfect. As everyone read this press release, a feeling of "Esprite De Corps" (Latin for the spirit of the corps) came over the group, as I hadn't seen since I was in the military. We all felt as though we were well armed, about to go in to battle. I felt empowered, and confident, and we could all smell a sense of justice that we had been hoping for so long. This would be the last time any of us would have this feeling, ever again.

As we sat there eating breakfast together, I realized what a tremendous amount of quality, and experience we had in the people that we were going to battle with. All of us were seasoned veterans who, prior to becoming whistle blowers, had immaculate careers, and high profile cases. For example: Sandy had the famous "Jewelry Mart" case that was previewed in News Week magazine; Mike Connor had several famous cases, and was interviewed on the T.V. news show 20/20; Tom Allison was a previous supervisor for Customs, with several record seizures, before leaving Customs and obtaining his law degree; Shannon Getz, prior FBI Agent, and survivor of the Oklahoma City Bombing; Ervin Rios, a highly decorated Senior Customs Inspector; John Carmon a highly decorated/respected former Customs Inspector; Cathy Harris, a highly decorated/respected Customs Inspector and soon to be published author; and Ruben and I who have both had record seizures, and high profile cases that were quoted in the media.

Mike Connor gave us a bit of juicy information about our nemesis Brinkley. He informed us that he and Brinkley had worked together for a while, and that he introduced Brinkley to his wife. The night that this introduction took place, Brinkley proceeded to take this woman (a civilian) in his G-ride, bar hopping. Oh how ironic. Here Brinkley was trying to stick Ruben with 45 days on the bricks for having his kids in Ruben's G-ride, while Brinkley himself had been out joy riding civilians on a bar hopping excursion all in his G-ride. Mike told us of how Stuart 'Stew' Peters, ex-Internal Affairs investigator had even better dirt on Brinkley involving an accidental discharge that was covered up. Evidently, when Brinkley was an agent in San Diego, he accidentally discharged his weapon. The round went right through the office window almost hitting two agents sitting at their desk. Under Customs policy Brinkley was to get a mandatory suspension and a red file. Instead, he got a promotion, compliments of the local IA supervisor who covered this up for Brinkley. Brinkley would later repay the favor for this manager by fraudulently ruling a vehicle accident that happened in a personal vehicle on personal time, as a work related accident. The Customs Quid-Pro-Quo method of management.

After breakfast, we all walked together from the Mission Inn, to the RAIC/Riverside, where we would take our stand. My husband Ben met us there with plenty of Arrowhead water for everyone. He's a good man. Ruben's family and kids were there. I thought about bringing my kids, but feared negative consequences of having them exposed to the media. I've always had this distrust/hatred of the media. I saw them as just a bunch of sharks that would sell their own mother for a story, and didn't care how accurate it was. I saw all journalists as tabloid, etch-a-sketchers, who if they couldn't get the real deal, they would just lift up the see-through page, and make it up as they go. I never gave journalists the time of day, and only gave information to the media when it suited my needs, or management forced me to. How ironic, here I was now putting my fate in the hands of the media. I felt my stomach burning as the news cameras and hand mikes began to appear.

I was selected as sort of an M.C. for this thing. I introduced Cathy Harris who gave a very Charismatic speech, and spoke of the abuse that she had to endure at the hands of this agency. I then introduced the local president of MAPA, the Mexican American Political Association. He gave an excellent supportive speech, and stated that MAPA was going to file an official complaint with Congress on our behaves. Then I introduced Ruben, who just about brought me to tears. I was very proud of Ruben that day, his speech was eloquent and dignified. And last but not least, I introduced Tom Allison who read the press release, and then answered questions.

The demonstration was well organized, professional, and we even had signs. Shannon Getz was afraid to make any speeches, but was interviewed by one of the reporters from the API News. I'll never forget what she said to this reporter, and how this statement put this whole thing in a deeper perspective for me. She told the reporter that because of the tremendous amount of pressure and retaliation put on her as a result of her whistle blowing, that becoming a whistle blower was more traumatic/horrific than surviving the Oklahoma City bombing. As Shannon softly, in almost a whisper of a voice, spoke these words, you could see the pain and fear exuding from her whole being. She had tears in her eyes, her voice was cracking, and she reminded me of a weak little kitten, about to be drowned.

I felt like the elephant was once again standing on my chest. I wanted so badly to hug her and show her compassion, but I didn't. Her words gave me a sense of fear, and dread that if I went to her, I might somehow contract her weaknesses, like contracting an illness. I pretended not to hear her, and made jokes with Ervin. From that day on, I found myself feeling uncomfortable around Shannon. I was afraid of becoming weak, and beaten down like her, much as the same way I feel uncomfortable around someone in a wheel chair; afraid that this too could happen to me, but not if I only keep my distance. I had developed this false sense of security that by distancing myself from others' weaknesses or things that scare me, this will somehow put up a magical force field, keeping me from their fate.

As I thought about this, and how I was feeling toward Shannon, and her weaknesses, I realized that what I was feeling, in a very real sense, was a sort of prejudice. Here I was, in the middle of a battle that was in part a battle to fight discrimination, and I realized that I had carried deep inside me, a prejudice; a very real prejudice against the weak and helpless. I knew that this personality trait of mine was born out of fear, and learned from early in my childhood. My fear of others' weaknesses and frailties had made me a less caring and compassionate person than I would like to have been. From that day on, and in spite of this self-awareness, I kept a translucent distance from Shannon, and often times, was not there for her when she needed me the most. I would regret this always.

The demonstration went O.K., but I was disappointed in the amount, and quality of coverage given to us by the media. We were quoted in newspapers across the country, and all quotes were buried in small columns, on the 4th or 5th page. I saw this as the media's way at getting back at me, for all of the arrogant, condescending remarks I had thrown their way, in lieu of the information they sought on my cases. When I went home that night, my husband was very proud of me. He told me that I did the right thing, standing up for Ruben and all. I wanted so badly to share with Ben my feelings, and fears about what Shannon Getz had said to the media, but I didn't. Ben was proud of me, and I was too chicken-shit to let him in on the real insensitive coward I had been toward Shannon. I was afraid of what he'd think of me. I drank a lot of milk that night, when I couldn't sleep.

The following day after this demonstration, Ruben and I had to face our other coworkers at the RAIC/Riverside. Yolanda Rios, as always, was very supportive and was filling us in on the reactions of the office during the demonstration. Evantie, of course, was embarrassed and pissed. As Yolanda told me of his reaction, I felt an extreme sense of a tiny taste of justice. Jerry Johnston smiled at me, and gave me a big hug. He said, "You stinker! I can't believe you guys did this! What incredible balls you guys have." Jerry loved seeing Evantie squirm, as did most everyone in the office.

Most people didn't agree with our course of action, but all liked to see Evantie squirm. I must admit, I got a total rush on hearing of how this affected Evantie. I told Ruben, "Good! Let that son of a bitch see how it feels to have the heat at his door." I was in this because I wanted to cause some kind of justice, but what I came to realize was that I also wanted to hurt and humiliate Evantie, and others like him in management. I kept thinking of the IA pukes reading me my rights like I was some kind of criminal, and how I was passed over for promotion by morons that couldn't investigate their way out of a paper bag. What I was also craving was revenge, something that I thought that I was immune to.

A couple of days after the demonstration, our new Group Supervisor, Lewis Cohen called me into his office. I thought to myself, oh no, here it goes, expecting some sort of retaliation. Then as I was coming down the hall he stated, bring your tanker car case with you. I gathered up my stuff and met him in his office. He asked me to brief him in detail, the whole history of the rail project, and on my criminal cases. I found him to be surprisingly supportive of me and of my concerns. As the conversation developed, I felt more and more comfortable speaking somewhat candidly about Evantie, and Brinkley's undermining of my case and of the rail project. I held back the information that Ervin Rios, Ruben, Renado, and I had dug up which pointed a corruption finger square at Brinkley's crooked face. I still saw Lewis as management, and therefore not to be trusted.

After briefing Lewis, he told me that he felt that I had done a good job on the project and the case so far. He shared with me that he too had gone up against Brinkley once, and came out on the short end of the stick. He told me that he thought that the rail project was a viable one, and that I should have been given more support. He stated, "Darlene, you're caught in the middle of a political machine. On one hand, no one else has the extensive knowledge, extensive training, or the interest in this rail stuff, and on the other hand, you've made one hell of a seizure, and gained important information into the Arellano-Felix Organization." Lewis further stated, "I want you to write a rail project, and I am going to try to ram-rod it through." I responded, "You mean rewrite it don't you? I already had the project written, and up and running when it was derailed by Brinkley, and we all know what that's all about now don't we?" Stephen laughed, "Derailed, ha that's a funny pun. Darlene, having a spine is not always popular, or politically correct for one's career, believe me, I know."

I stared into his eyes with distrust and curiosity as I was trying to size him up. What was his angle? Why was he acting like he was going to help me? Why would he go up against Brinkley after he had seen what had happened to us? Lewis was new, had only been at the office for a couple of weeks, and I had yet to size him up. He looked back into my eyes as if to sense that I was sizing him up, distrusting him. Then he paused, sighed, and said, "Look, take what you've done, update it, and put it in the new project proposal format. Darlene, I'm not your enemy here. I believe in this project and I'm going to help you get past the political stumbling blocks that are currently in your way." I asked him, "Even if that mean's going up against Brinkley?" He responded, "I did it once, and I'm not afraid to do it again." We both sat there glaring at each other, trying to read each others mind, looking for a flinch or some tell-tale sign to figure each other out. Finally, I took a deep breath, got up, and said, "O.K., you got it. First draft will be on your desk by tomorrow morning." Lewis responded, "Hey, wow. I don't expect you to have this done by tomorrow. Take a week at least." I responded in my determined "Captains" tone of voice, "You'll have it on your desk tomorrow sir."

Lewis started laughing, and in a sweet tone of voice said, "Darlene, sit back down here for a minute and talk to me, just let's talk, O.K.?" I paused for a minute and sat back down. Lewis said, "Look, I understand agents like you and Jerry. You're not like the rest of these guys, you're military background and brainwashing is a big part of you. I know, I was a Naval Officer. I know how you guys think, duty and honor above all else. Hell, I admire that in you. Still, you've got to play politics sometimes, everyone does." There was a long pause. I just sat there looking at him with this expression of "why in the hell is he telling me this?" Then Lewis said, "So how's the Olympics training going? I know you were working hard on cutting your time on your flip turns. Did you ever get Mike to work with you on that?" I said, "Yea, he showed me a better technique for coming off the wall that not only cut time, but relieved the pressure on my shoulder injury." We continued with small talk, with him trying to win my trust with a display of interest and concern about me proceeding with my training with injuries. Then he asked me if I could put together a meeting with the Federal prosecutor, and the powers that be with the Customs Inspectors, and the locals involved in the rail project. I told him that I thought that was a good idea, and that I'd see to it. The next day at 1100hrs, I placed the draft of the "new improved" rail project on his desk with a note telling him that the meeting would be at the U.S. Attorney's office on Monday morning at 0900hrs.

I had lunch with Ruben and Renado the next day at the usual dive, and briefed them on the warm and fuzzy I had with Lewis. They weren't sure what to think of it, but Renado committed to be at the rail meeting. Renado said, "Don't worry guys, I'll get a fix on this and point this boy Lewis in the right direction." Then Renado said, "By the way woman, you are looking mighty fine. All that swimming and running is slimmed you way down." Ruben said, "Don't be encouraging her Renado. She doesn't look fine, she's way too thin, and she looks like a weakling. She's obsessed with this running and swimming business." I looked at Ruben and said, "Kiss my grits Ruben." Ruben fired back, "Hey, she didn't cuss." I flicked an ice cube down his shirt.

On Monday morning, most of the parties involved in the rail project met. Lewis, Ervin, Renado, Yvette, and Chief O'Leary were there. We made small talk at first, and then Yvette point blank asked Lewis who was torpedoing the rail project. Lewis answered, in front of everyone, "Drake Brinkley." Then Yvette asked him why, and he didn't have an answer. Yvette looked at me with great concern, and then looked back at Lewis with great suspicion. We did some brainstorming, and Lewis handed out my second version of the new "Operation Lite Rail" proposal.

After the meeting, Renado, Ervin and I stayed behind to meet with Yvette. I updated Renado and Yvette on the suspicions and information Ervin and I had put together. Renado looked at Yvette and said, "Do you want to know what I think? I'll tell you what I think. Darlene stumbled into some shit here." Renado looked at me and said, "You weren't supposed to find that loaded tanker car, and they certainly don't want you over there finding another one. Do you know what else? I think this Brinkley guy is crooked as hell, and all of you guys are in danger." Yvette's face showed great concern, and even fear as she listened. I looked at Renado and said, "What do you mean, you guys? You've been in the middle of this since day one palley-boy; if they miss me, the bullet will probably hit you."

The next day former Customs Inspector and well-publicized San Diego whistleblower, John Carmon told us of an FBI agent out of San Diego, that was already looking into the border corruption issues related to the Hydro tanker car seizure. Carmon suggested that we all go talk to him. I got his name and number, and made an appointment to see him

Ervin Rios, Sandy Nun, Ruben Sandoval, Clark Janice, John Carmon and I met with FBI Special Agent William Motts. We briefed him on everything that we had put together thus far, and the guy just seemed totally overwhelmed. We also told him of the added fear that we had of how these tanker cars could be easily used by terrorists as the perfect instruments to deliver weapons of mass destruction. Ruben and I explained to him of how one could turn these things into the world's largest pipe bombs. It is not a quantum leap to think that the same modus opporandi used by narco traffickers, could easily be used by terrorists to deliver bombs or biological / chemical agents. One wouldn't even have to use a suicide bomber. These tanker cars could be sent to a hundred different rail spurs (much in the same way that the drug smugglers did) all across the U.S., and then activated remotely. You'd never be able to track the terrorist. These rail accounts can be set up easily with phony I.D. and cash with no check or balance system in Customs or in the rail customer service industry. We told the FBI Agent that this was a recipe for disaster. The whole time that we were briefing him he had this bewildered look on his face as if to say, oh no, this looks like too much work and a political nightmare. I knew by the way that he reacted to us, that he was going to somehow weasel out of doing anything. He wasn't taking any notes, and seemed to not take what we were explaining to him, very seriously.

Ten days after the demonstration, Ruben got called into Evantie's office, with Lewis in tow, and Evantie read Brinkley's proposal to give Ruben 45 days on the bricks. I was at the gym working out when I got the page. Ruben was livid, and rightfully so. We met at the usual dive with Renado. Ruben was visibly worried. He knew that this would kill him financially, and he just had a new little baby boy. Renado and I tried to console him.

The next day, I walked into the office and passed by David Gray. Looked at him briefly and said hey. He looked back at me with a demonic expression. I knew that his IA thug buddies had already clued him in on his impending attempted rape investigation. I immediately regretted leaving my gun in the trunk of my G-ride. I sat at my desk working on reports, and waited for the hammer to drop. Gray passed by my doorway, and from the hallway outside my wall he hit my wall so hard, that one of my pictures fell off. Ruben wasn't there, and I was getting scared, and angry.

After a few minutes, Gray pounded on my wall again. I thought he was going to put his fist through it. I had a tennis racquet next to my desk. My fear turned to rage, and I felt my blood boiling in my veins. I took the racquet and walked down the hall towards Gray's office. I swung the racket against the medal frame on his door. Gray was startled, and jumped in his chair. I looked at him with an arrogant challenging glare. I said in a low, deliberate tone of voice, "Oh. Sorry Gray, am I disturbing you?" He looked at me a bit startled, and looked back at his computer and ignored me. I got a hold of my temper, and walked back to my office. My chest was pounding, and my face was hot.

A little while later, Ruben walked in. I told him what had just happened. He walked over to me, squatted down next to my chair, and whispered to me in a firm tone of voice, "Now you better listen to me you little wench, you had better start carrying your p-shooter. I mean it. I don't want to see you any more unarmed. That crazy bastard Gray is likely to do anything, and I don't want to see you get hurt. If I let you get hurt, Ben will kill me." I smiled at him and in a munchkin sounding tone of voice I said, "Oh little man don't worry, I have a tennis racquet." Ruben rose up and said, "Give me that," and grabbed the tennis racquet away from me. I made a fish face at him, and he couldn't help laughing. He shook his head at me holding back a grin, and I could see the concern on his face.

That night the dream returned. I was standing in the Daniel Boon National Forest on a trail overlooking the waterfalls at Cumberland Falls State Park. I immediately recognized this place. This was one of my most favorite places growing up. I used to sit for hours listening to the relaxing sound of the water as it flowed over the falls. As I would watch the water go over the falls, it was mesmerizing. Here I was again, feeling the cool rocks on the overhang above my head. The air was fresh, cool and crisp. Everything was so brilliantly colored with the colors of fall. It was beautiful, and I never wanted to leave there again. I looked down the all-too-familiar trail, and saw the toddler standing there. He was still filthy, and starred at me with his big, deep blue eyes and melted my heart. I walked toward him, and he smiled. I knew he was about to take me somewhere else and I spoke to him, "Please let us stay here for just a little while." He smiled in an impish little way, and then I was somewhere else.

We were at the farm again. The toddler took me by the hand, and I picked him up. I walked to the top of the small hill, and could see the farm at the other side of the hill. I immediately looked to find the corral. There he was, the strange young man. He was sitting on the back of an old flat bed truck. The bed of the truck and the side railings were made of wooden planks. It reminded me of an old truck that my grandfather had. He used it to take feed to the cows and horses. I could only see the young man at a slanted rear view, through the wooden planks. He was dressed the same, was smoking, and slightly dangling his boots back and forth. On the tailgate next to him, he had a Styrofoam cup of tea. I could see the tea bag tag hanging out of the cup. I heard him talking in his strange accent. His voice was deep and soft. He was talking to the ducks and chickens. He had something he was feeding them. I looked to see if there were any humans near by, and he was clearly only talking to the ducks and chickens. He seemed relaxed and at peace with himself, not at all how he was in my dream of him at the Shrine Auditorium. This is where he belonged. I took a deep breath, and noticed how beautiful everything was, and noticed that I too was at peace with myself. I walked closer, and to the side of the truck in an effort to see his face. Something stopped me, and I felt frustration. I could see only the side of his face through the wooden planks. I saw his eyes again; eyes that could intoxicate you, deep blue like the ocean. I wanted to yell to him, or get his attention, and I couldn't. In a split second, I was awake.

I lay there pondering this. Why was I dreaming this? What did 'this mean? If this was that angel of death, why was he smoking, and talking to poultry? If this was some type of message, why didn't anyone ever talk to me? Was I supposed to purchase stock in poultry and tea today? Why was the toddler always dirty, and pitiful looking? Why couldn't I ever see the man's face? Why was it that every time I started feeling relaxed and at peace with myself, that little toddler jerked me somewhere else, or I awoke? I tried to put this out of my mind for fear of going insane. I was afraid of telling anyone about these dreams for fear that this information might get into the wrong hands. The enemy (corrupt Customs managers and IA) would have a field day with something like this so that they could say that I was nuts, and use it against me to attack my credibility. I could just imagine Evantie laughing in my face as he took my badge and gun and put me on stress leave because of my dreams. I would never give him that satisfaction.

May 25, 1999, I got a call from Sandy Nunn. She told me that they had just called her in and gave her a letter of disciplinary action, which included three days on the bricks, beginning today. She was so angry, but had the intelligence to see that this was only proving our point, and making our future litigation easier. I talked to her and her mom later that evening. I could tell that her mom was getting very worried. I felt sorry for Sandy's mom, and was glad that I had decided not to tell my parents anything about what was going on. I had heard the concern in Sandy's mom's voice, and as a parent, I completely understood and empathized with her.

Chapter 23

Another Surprise

May 26, 1999, Sandy and I had lunch with ex-Customs Special Agent Ron Bundy. Ron was one of the first people that I met when I swore in with Customs. Ron had recently retired after suffering similar abuses that we were suffering, at the hands of Drake Brinkley. Ron was a fraud and money laundering expert that used to work on a large U.C. project with David Gray. Over lunch Sandy and I filled him in on what had been happening to us, and the roll that David Gray had been playing. Ron responded, "None of this surprises me at all Darlene. Don't you get it? David Gray is crazy about you, and has been for years." I said, "What? Where are you getting this from? No Way." Ron said, "Don't you remember that Christmas Party several years ago at the U.C. (undercover) off sight. Do you remember that someone stole one of your shoes, a red pump? It was Gray. For two weeks after that party, all any of us ever heard about from him was, 'Oh Darlene' this, and 'Oh Darlene' that. He couldn't stop talking about you, and how great you looked in your red dress and shoes. That nut carried your shoe around for days, and kept it on his desk. We all thought he was loco."

I was in shock. I had no Idea. I told Ron, "Ron, none of this makes sense. Gray's happily married." Ron said, "I'm telling you Darlene, married or not, this guy is obsessed with you. Don't you remember how he was trying so hard to get you assigned to the U.C. project permanently? And if he hadn't gotten transferred to IA, with his pull he would have gotten his way. Why he even told everyone that's why he was putting in to return back to RAIC/Riverside; to work with you, the infamous

Darlene." I said, "Well, I was wondering why he made it a point to move into the same office as Ruben and I." Ron responded, "Exactly. He fully expected that you and he would partner up because of your previous friendship, and that he would worm his way into a relationship with you. Then when he was sent to do management's dirty work on Ruben, you did the unexpected. You stood up for Ruben against Gray." I said, "I stood up for the truth, and defended my partner against discrimination and retaliation." Ron said, "Yeah, but that's not how Gray sees it. He sees it as you and he go way back, before Ruben. He thought that since you were so close, you would naturally side with him against Ruben; and when you didn't, Gray saw it as a betrayal."

Sandy said, "You know this all makes perfect sense. I knew that Gray always acted like a jilted lover around you." I responded, "Jilted lover! This is bullshit. We were only friends. The man never even made a serious pass at me, he knew how I felt about loathing married men who cheat." Ron Said, "Trust me Darlene, Gray would have picked and chose his timing carefully. Then he would have found you at a vulnerable moment, and wormed his way into your life. Believe me Dar, this guy sees Ruben as the guy that stole you away from him." I said, "Ron! This doesn't make any sense. Ruben and I are happily married, and we've never even contemplating having any type of romantic relationship. This is crazy!" Ron said, "No it's not Dar. That's your perception. Gray doesn't know the relationship that you and Ruben have, he only knows that you dumped him for Ruben." Sandy shook her head in agreement and said, "Darlene I've seen how David Gray looks at you. He's in love with you and he blames Ruben for turning you against him." Ron pointed at Sandy, shook his head yes, and said, "Exactly. Face it Darlene, Gray has it in for Ruben, and it's more than just doing the dirty work for management."

I went home that night in total shock. Had I been that naive that I didn't see this? Had I misjudged Gray's feelings about me all along? And what if they were right. Poor Ruben! I felt so guilty. I felt like Ruben was on the receiving end of Gray's revenge because of me. I told my husband what Ron and Sandy had told me, and much to my surprise, Ben responded, "That doesn't surprise me at all honey. You remember, I was at several of these parties, and I too saw how Gray acted around you. They're right, it's obvious." I said, "How in the hell did I miss this one? I'm supposed to be a trained investigator, what's wrong with me?"

Ben said, "Darlene, when it comes to these things, you are a bit naive. You don't realize how you look, and the effect that you have on men. I mean, you reeled me in didn't you?" Then Ben tickled me and got me to laugh with him. Then Ben said, "Don't worry Dar, Ruben's a big boy. He doesn't hold you responsible for Gray's behavior, Ruben's smarter than that. You and Ruben just keep sticking together, no matter what."

Chapter 24

The Ultimate Price

On May 28, 1999, I got a 911 page from Sandy. I called her back and she was hysterical. She told me that her dad had just died of a heart attack. Sandy was crushed. Sandy and her dad Rocky were very close. Rocky Nunn was a veteran Air Force pilot, and a 20yr veteran of the Immigrations Service. Rocky was a well known, well respected, and loved man. My heart ached for Sandy and her mom Jean. Rocky and Jean had been married for close to 50 years.

Ruben, Ervin, Shannon and I all attended the funeral. Rocky was buried with full military honors, and a formal salute from the Border Patrol. Sandy's poor mom looked so shattered and frail, and Sandy's face displayed the look of an anguished, broken heart. My heart ached for them both. After the funeral, we went to lunch and Sandy told me that her mom had said that Rocky was so worried about what was going on with Sandy being retaliated against. On of the things that Rocky told Jean was that he felt helpless. He said, "I'm old, and weak and I can't help my daughter." Jean relayed that Rocky was in despair when he was told of Sandy's suspension resulting from the Customs IA investigation. I went home that night, called my dad, laughed with him, and told him that I loved him. Of all the things that had happened to all of us, this was the straw that broke the camels back. This wonderful man lost his life worrying about his daughter suffering at the hands of men of the likes of Drake Brinkley. This price was too high to pay. Sandy later went back to her father's grave and vowed to Rocky that she wouldn't stop fighting the system, until justice was done.

I had been training hard for the Police Olympics, and all too quick, it was here. It was the 2nd and 3rd week of June 1999, and I had entered three events; a cross-country 10k run, and two swimming events. The 10k took place on equestrian trails at a park in Pasadena, CA. When the race began, I knew we had problems when the sign read "Advanced Riders Only." It was one of the toughest cross-country courses I had ever run. It reminded me of being back in the military where things made sense. It was challenging and fun, and I survived it.

The swimming events took place at the Aquatic Center, in Pasadena, CA. My first event was at 0900 that morning. I had to commute 2 hours to the location, and got there an hour before check in. I hardly slept the night before, nervous and anxious about the events. It was cold that morning, and I couldn't seem to get warmed up. I completed my first event, and laid down on one of the benches. I fell fast asleep, as the sun came out warming my cold, tired body. I awoke suddenly to them calling my next event. The other swimmers were already behind the blocks. I ran over to the event sign-in table, and forgot my event card. I was still half asleep, and ran back to get my card. When I got to my block, the other swimmers were already there looking at me in disapproval for making them wait. The loud speaker said, "Swimmers take your mark." I jumped up on to the block, and got into position. Then the loud speaker said, "Stand down, stand down. Lane seven, would you remove your sun glasses please." I then noticed that all the other swimmers were laughing at me, and I realized that they were talking to me. I stepped down, removed my glasses, and put my goggles on. I felt like such a bonehead.

I ended up taking two silver medals in the Police Olympics. The following Monday, Brinkley put out an SAIC/LA office wide e-mail message congratulating everyone who took medals at the police Olympics. Everyone's name was listed but mine. I thought of just how childish this was. I told myself it didn't matter, that I didn't compete for them anyway, that I was just trying to set a good example for my kids, and make them proud. But it hurt. When Ruben got into the office, I showed him my medals. He gave me a big hug and told me he was proud of me. Then Jerry Johnston walked in, saw the medals, and Hi5vd me. I told them about how I made a fool of myself by forgetting to remove my sunglasses on the blocks, and they both cracked up. I later showed Ruben the e-mail from the SAIC office. He couldn't believe it. He said, "Man, that's low. What a bunch of idiots!" I told him that it was no big deal, and I tried to conceal my hurt, but I know he knew.

Later that morning we had an office meeting. Jerry congratulated me in front of everyone. Ruben was pissed off and I could tell that he was about to say something, so I kicked him in the shins under the table, and subtly shook my head no. Lewis acted impressed, and sincerely congratulated me, as did several others. Evantie just sat there, glared at me with a condescending smirk, and refused to in any way recognize my accomplishments. I fantasized about choking him to death, with my bare hands. I could see his face turning white, and feel the life draining out of him. I caught myself staring at him as I was thinking this, and I noticed he was looking back wondering what I was about to say or do. I took a deep breath, got up and walked out of the meeting. My rage and thoughts scared me, and I knew this was all designed to bait me, the "Hot Head," and I knew that I had better not react. I knew that if I ever really lost it, I would be out of control, and that's just the type of ammunition they'd need to fire me, or worse.

On July 18, 1999, I received a response from Customs Regional EEO Complaint center, on one of the EEO complaints of retaliation that I had previously filed. Contained therein, was a statement from EEO Supervisor, Mary Conales stating that it was in fact she who in 1997, turned my EEO file (containing Sandy's statement) over to IA. Here it was two years later, and she was admitting this. For two years, Conales had conveniently omitted the fact that she did this. She had made two sworn statements dissuading that what we were receiving could have been retaliation, since there was no way that, at the time, management could have known about our complaints. I showed this to Ruben and he immediately recognized the significance of this. At the time that Conales turned my packet over to IA, Elaine Black was the head of IA, and her second in command was Stella O'Shea, wife of Dudley O'Shea. Dudley O'Shea and Drake Brinkley were big buds, and Elaine Black became, and was currently the ASAIC (Assistant Special Agent in Charge) under Brinkley. Additionally, this leak happened while David Gray was working in IA Therein lies the much-needed nexus of how management knew full well who was filing complaints, and thus the retaliation. When I faxed this to our attorney Tom, he said that it was golden, and that Conales was toast.

On July 20, 1999, Ruben and I were in the office completing reports. Lewis came to the doorway and said, "Ruben. Evantie and I need to see you in Evantie's office." Ruben and I looked at each other with dread, and we both knew that this was going to be Ruben's sentencing for his 45-day suspension without pay. Ruben looked at Lewis and said, "I'm not going in there without a witness," and as he stood up he said, "Let's go Dar." I took my weapon off, and locked it up in my drawer, for fear of loosing my temper. We all walked into Evantie's Office as Evantie sat there looking at a document with this smug, egomaniac look on his face. I wanted so badly to kick that chair out from under him, and wipe that smirk off his face. I thought it would be more than justice for Evantie's ego to have his but kicked by a girl. I caught myself dreaming about beating him up in front of everybody.

Evantie told us to sit down. Ruben and Lewis sat down, and I took up a firm, almost military (at ease) standing position against the door. This was a small act of defiance on my part. Evantie began reading Ruben's letter of suspension. With each condescending word out of Evantie's mouth, I could see Ruben's knuckles turning white, as he was squeezing the arms on his chair. I was somewhat surprised at Lewis' reaction. He was visibly disgusted with this, and was throwing Evantie some pretty disrespectful looks. Had I underestimated him? Evantie then asked for

Ruben's badge, weapon, and keys. The look on Ruben's face was a combination of rage, disbelief, and helplessness. All I felt was rage. Ruben
coughed up his badge and gun, and said, "My keys are at my desk."
Evantie looked at me and said, "Can you go get them for us Dar?" I stood
there glaring at Evantie, and he knew that I wanted to kill him. I was
truly looking into the face of an extreme narcissist; the most uncompas-
sionate, Hitler, son of a bitch I'd ever met. He was truly enjoying this.

Just then Evantie said condescendingly, "Ah Dar, the keys." I took a
deep breath, and Lewis, anticipating that I was about to do something
stupid, stood up and gently placed his hand on my arm. Lewis was
talking to Ruben and looking into my eyes at the same time, and said
"Ruben, I'll show you how to file an appeal on this in my office." As
Lewis said "In my office" he squeezed my arm as if to subtly say, don't
do this, come with me, we'll handle this. I looked Lewis in the eyes,
took a deep breath, and subtly nodded my head up and down, as if to
acknowledge an attempt at trust. Ruben got up, looked at Lewis and
said, "You know this is bullshit, don't you?" Lewis looked at Evantie
with a look of agreement with Ruben and said, "Common guys, lets go
to my office and talk." Evantie looked at Lewis with the disgusted look
of betrayal.

We left Evantie's office, and started down the hall. I stopped in the
office foyer by the sign-in/sign-out board. I looked at Ruben, and could
see that anger and worry on his face. I felt helpless that there was nothing I could do to help him. I was afraid I might start crying, and refused
to let anyone, especially Evantie, see this. Lewis said, "Where you
going?" I responded, "I'll catch you later, Ruben, I'll be back in a bit and
drive you home." I signed out, and drove over to the UP (Union Pacific)
rail yard, in Colton.

I sat on the hill overlooking the rail yard, and watched the tanker cars
moving onto the hump to be weighed. My mind was racing, and my
blood was boiling. I was sure that this rail car stuff was what all this was
really all about. Renado had been right from the beginning, and Ruben

and I didn't see it soon enough. I felt so bad for Ruben; I knew how bad this would hit him financially. I kept replaying Evantie's arrogance in my mind, over and over again. My stomach was killing me, burning all the way up my throat. I drove to a Jack N The Box to get a milk shake for my stomach. As I drove through the drive through window, I remembered how it was Ruben who taught me that in Spanish Jack In The Box was Joaquin en La caja. I didn't want to go back to the office, but I wanted to be the one to drive Ruben home. I knew that's what he would want, and he deserved this loyalty.

As I pulled back into the parking garage of our office, there he was, Evantie. Hitler himself, walking toward his G-ride. A very dark thought came over me. I imagined myself gunning my engine, and running over Evantie. My rage boiled inside my burning stomach. I saw the act of running him over as stomping out pure evil incarnate. I felt my hands tighten on the steering wheel, and my chest pounding. Just then I was startled by someone beeping their horn behind me. I took a deep breath shook my head, looked back towards Evantie, and he had made it to his car. He'll never know how close he came.

On the way to Ruben's house, neither one of us hardly spoke. I tried to reassure him that everything was going to work out, and that he had a lot of people who cared for him and would somehow show their loyalty. I fumbled around with trying to show some compassion, and did a miserable job of it. I was never any good at showing the compassion that was truly in my heart. In any attempt at being soft or compassionate with adults, I would have this strange embarrassing feeling come over me, as though the wind had blown my skirt up in front of a group full of people, and I had stupid embarrassing underwear on. The only time that I didn't feel like this; the only time I felt comfortable showing compassion or being soft, was with my kids.

The 45 days that Ruben was gone were tough. Either Lewis and/or AUSA Yvette must have put pressure on someone, because suddenly, I was back on the rail project. On August 2, 1999 I had put in for the

Customs Physical Fitness Specialist School, at the Cooper Clinic, in Dallas Texas. Two days later, I got my memo back with Evantie's handwriting on it stating that Brinkley wasn't sending anyone. When I submitted my request, I also sent my memo to the Regional Fitness Director, Peter Blake. Blake had called me back upon receiving my memo, and told me that there were several funded positions, and he had submitted my application to Headquarters. What a contradiction.

Several days later, my school selection packet came from headquarters. I showed Lewis the memo from Evantie, the memo from Blake, and the packet I'd received from headquarters. I knew this was putting Lewis in one hell of a spot, but I needed to know if I could trust him or not, and this would be a good test. I told Lewis of how several years ago his predecessor Ivan Winkowsky had chiseled me out of this school before. I told him how schools were scarce then and I had to compete for the school based on my background and experience. I was selected most qualified not only at the RAIC level, but was selected most qualified for the entire SAIC office. I told Lewis of how none of this mattered, and Winkowsky ordered me to give up my slot to his office kiss ass and good old boy, Edwin Easel, who hadn't even qualified to make the list for any of the slots.

Lewis looked at me with sympathy, and seemed sincere when he said, "Dar, I'm going to take care of this, and this time you will be going." A couple of hours later, Lewis poked his head in my door and said, "Pack your bags, you are going to Dallas." Later that day Yolanda Rios (office Investigative Assistant) told me about how she could hear Lewis in Evantie's office, and they were arguing about something regarding me. I felt a new sense of trust of Lewis, and it felt good. At this point, there were only a select few people I felt I could trust, and the RAIC/Riverside was a pretty grim place to walk in to. I knew that Evantie would see the act of Lewis defending me, as a betrayal. I knew that Evantie would blame me for that betrayal, and would view it as an "end-run" around him. I knew Evantie would have to get even, and again put me in my place.

The day before I left for Dallas to the fitness school, we had an office meeting. Lewis mentioned that I was going to be gone for a week to the fitness school and Evantie arrogantly responded, "Well I hope you don't come back here thinking that you're gonna try and whip us into shape or anything." I looked at him, and noticed his pack of cigarettes lying on the table in front of him (Lawrence Evantie was a chain smoker). I pushed the cigarettes toward him and in a condescending tone of voice said, "No Lawrence, I'm gonna come back here and buy you a carton of cigarettes." Everyone laughed, and Evantie was pissed off that I'd embarrassed him. Even though I knew that he'd make me pay for this somehow, I just couldn't help myself. Then Evantie made a rather interesting announcement. He stated that Brinkley had reiterated an earlier policy, and was intent on avidly enforcing it. This policy demanded that all agents utilize regular gas in their G-rides, as apposed to the more expensive high-grade/super unleaded gases. Evantie further stated, "You all know how 'hands-on' Brinkley is when it comes to vehicles." I kicked Ruben under the table, and we smiled at each other. This was in direct contradiction to what Brinkley had testified to, under oath, in the deposition for Ruben's civil case. Brinkley, under oath, stated that he had nothing to do with vehicles and that anything to do with vehicles was assigned to someone else. We knew all along that Brinkley lied under oath, but now we had a room full of witnesses as to what Evantie had just stated.

Chapter 25

Twisting The Knife

I left the next day for a wonderful, peaceful week in Dallas. The humidity was a bitch, but I was able to put Customs out of my mind if only just for a while. The Monday that I returned, I signed on to check my e-mail first thing. There was a message from headquarters congratulating the top three "SPS" (Significant Problem Solving) Projects. Operation Lite Rail (my rail project) won an award for one of the best projects of the year. Then they listed the names of all the Customs employees who had participated. Each participant was to receive a Commissioner's Citation, and $1000.00. Everyone on the project was listed but me, and there was no reference to all the work AUSA Yvette had done either. As I read this, I was in shock, and I could feel a sinking sensation in my heart and my stomach burned up through my throat. This wasn't just a knife in the back; this was twisting the already existing knife for a final death of my spirit, which quickly turned to pure unadulterated rage.

I printed out the message, grabbed it, and stormed past Yolanda's desk to Evantie's office. I was going to cram the message down the son of a bitch's throat. I could feel the adrenaline running through my body, my face, feet and hands, felt hot. My chest was pounding, and I was truly out of control. I slammed my fist on Evantie's door. I suddenly noticed Yolanda and Lewis standing next to me, and she was saying, "He's gone, he's gone." Lewis asked me what was wrong, and I threw the memo at him, turned to Yolanda and said, "Where's that fucker at Yolanda, where's he at?" Yolanda was taken a-back, and didn't answer. I ran to her desk, and flipped through Evantie's appointment book. It displayed that he was on leave for a week. I went to my office, grabbed my keys, and signed out on the board for annual leave. Lewis tried to talk to me as I was signing out. He said, "Dar, I hope you know that I had nothing to do with this." I ignored him, and l walked out.

I went home called my husband and began crying. I was crying so hard, I wasn't making sense to him, and he was worried. All of the anger, frustration and helplessness of two years of emotional abuse was coming to the surface. I felt like I couldn't get control of my emotions, and stop crying. I had watched people that I cared about be harassed, humiliated, beaten down for two years. I was glad that Evantie wasn't present, or I would most certainly be sitting in jail right now. I called in sick the next day and began looking for another job.

On September 1, 1999, Sandy Nunn resigned in disgust from the U.S. Customs Service. The day that she resigned, we celebrated. She seemed totally free, felt great about her decision, and I envied her. She had secured a good position in private industry, and this inspired me to do the same. At her going away luncheon, I presented her a placket from the ACEC that stated, "for demonstrating courage against insurmountable odds." How appropriate those words were. I was proud of her.

On September 15, 1999, I completed my second interview with a solid company in private industry, and was selected. On September 16th, I submitted my letter of resignation with two weeks notice to my supervisor Lewis. He was in total shock and disbelief. He tried vigorously to talk me out of it to no avail. When I walked back to my office, Ruben was waiting for me. He already knew what I had decided to do. He and I had spoken several times about the company that I was interviewing with, and he was happy for me. I sat down, and showed him the letter.

As he was reading the letter of resignation, Jerry Johnston walked in and said, "What's going on folks?" I showed him the letter; he dropped down into a chair, and began to cry. He tried to talk me out of it, to no avail. He gave me a big hug, and said, "I'm gonna miss you. Who's gonna give me a hard time, and keep me straight around here?" I felt like a captain abandoning his loyal crew. I felt like I had failed, and was running away from a fight. Later that day I began to box things up from my desk, and take down my photos from my wall. I took the photo from the tanker car case, where I was on top of the car waving at everyone. I walked it over to Ruben and hung it on his bulletin board. I said to him, "Hey pizano, if you miss me, just look at me waving at you here in this picture." Ruben had tears in his eyes, and he gave me a big hug. He said, "God how I wish I was going with you Dar, you lucky thing you."

Chapter 26

Letting Go, and Moving On

On September 24, 1999, I walked into Evantie's office for the last time. Lewis was with me as I turned in my badge, weapon, and bulletproof vest. As I laid my badge on the table, I felt numb. I didn't feel the joy that Sandy displayed, I didn't feel rage, and I didn't feel sadness. I felt nothing. The badge that for so many years meant justice and honor to me, now lay on Evantie's table as a badge of dishonor, tarnished by managers like Drake Brinkley, Lawrence Evantie, and Harrison Wells. I felt like I was dreaming all of this; like I was asleep and my body was on autopilot performing these functions like an android. Lewis tried one more time to talk me out of it, and I politely ignored him.

Ruben and Jerry walked me down to Ruben's car to take me home. We stopped at the rear of the car, and Jerry put his hands in his pockets, looked at me in disbelief and said, "So that's it huh?" I looked at him and smiled and said, "That's it." Jerry hung his head, looked at the ground, and struggled for words. He shook his head and said, "Darlene, don't do this. Let's just walk back up-stairs, get your stuff and go catch bad guys." I looked into his eyes and they began tearing up. I put my hand out to shake his. He grabbed my hand, and pulled me into a long hug. As we hugged he said, "I'm gonna miss you my Kentucky gal." I gave him a tight squeeze, quickly turned and got into the car. As Ruben drove me away, I looked back at Jerry standing there in the garage watching us go. He stood there watching as if he was hoping that the car was going to stop, and we would turn around and I'd come back to work with him. He looked so pitiful, and I felt like I'd let him down.

Ruben and I talked only about my new job and how lucky I was to start my new life away from Customs. He was happy for me, and was trying to make this trip home easy for both of us. When he dropped me off, he helped me unload all of my stuff I had brought home from the office. I could sense his extreme discomfort about the situation. Ruben, much like me, had a real problem expressing any emotion other than rage. He had been my partner for 7 years now, through thick and thin, good and bad, and it was ending.

He gave me a quick hug, told me he would call me tomorrow, and jumped into his car and sped off. He was running away from his emotions, in the same manner that I had done so many times. I knew that he was hurting, and that he was feeling that I had left him behind and alone against Evantie and Brinkley. But I also knew that he understood that this was something that I just had to do, not just for me, but also for my family. My family needed a whole person, not some physically shattered woman in a rage every day. My husband and kids deserved better, and I was going to give it to them.

I often thought about what I'd miss most about the job, and it was the people. I missed my old mentor and surrogate father Bob Mattivi, who always took time from his busy schedule to guide me in the right direction with his good judgment, and lighten up the mood with his wit. I missed Jerry Johnston, my fellow kindred spirit from Kentucky. Jerry was always so gentile and soft-spoken, and added calmness to any situation; something a type A personality like me usually needed. He always seemed to understand me more than anyone else in the office. Our backgrounds were so similar. I missed Yolanda the Investigative Aid. She was like a surrogate big sister to me, always watching my back. She truly is a super lady. I had more laughs with her and Bob than I probably would have for the rest of my life. I missed my partner Ruben, my best friend, only second to my husband Ben. He was like a big brother to me, and made this job seem easy. I missed Renado. I missed all of his jokes and kidding around, but most of all I missed that kind of

Noble loyalty. It was like we were all a family, and I was being forced to move away from my home.

That night I dreamed again. I was in my old Customs office (the original office when I came to work in Riverside) talking to Jerry, Ruben, and Mattivi. We were joking and laughing, and I felt warm and loved inside. I looked down the hallway and there stood the toddler. I didn't recognize him at first. This time he was clean and beautiful. He was healthy, happy and smiled at me. I walked to him and picked him up. He smelled wonderful. He had that distinct "baby smell," like my kids use to smell when they were babies. I took a deep breath of him and closed my eyes. When I opened my eyes we were back on the beautiful farm. I now somehow felt that I was definitely in a foreign place. Everything was beautiful, and brightly colored. The green grass waved in the wind, and I could feel the cool spring-like breeze on my face. I put the toddler down, and we walked to the top of the small hill. There the farm lay in the beautiful little valley, with cows grazing on the nearby pastures. I heard the young man's deep, soft voice say, "Hello mates" in his British/Australian accent.

I looked to the left, and walking towards us from the old pick-up truck was the handsome young man I'd seen so many times before, but this time his back was not toward me. He was slowly walking towards us, with this cute "the cat's out of the bag; you caught me" smile. His eyes were beautiful blue, and gleamed like the ocean. The toddler took my hand, looked up at me smiling as if to say, go on, it's O.K. I walked toward the young man, and as I got closer I felt more and more at peace with myself. I felt light, and free. I felt as though I had known him all my life, like a long lost friend you were so happy to find. It was strange though. I had no romantic or passionate feelings toward him, this wasn't a romantic or sexual thing. It was as if I was looking into the face of a beautiful male angel, who came to lift me up, and put peace back into my heart.

The young man gently took my hand, looked into my eyes very shyly, and smiled. He led me to the back of the pick up truck, picked me up and sat me down on the bed of the truck. He jumped up, and sat down next to me. He had on a flannelled shirt, with a green T-shirt underneath, and cowboy boots. The truck began to move, as our feet dangled over the edge. As the truck rolled gently down the hill toward the pond, my tummy tickled from the movement, and we both laughed. I had no idea who was driving the truck, and didn't care. I felt implicit trust in the young man; trust that I had all but lost in humans in the real world.

The truck stopped at the pond, and backed up with the rear of the truck facing the pond. The young man looked at the pond, and the ducks, turned to me and said, "Isn't this beautiful?" I shook my head yes and smiled. The ducks had swum over to us, and he gave me some breadcrumbs to feed them. We sat there in total peace and tranquility for what seemed like hours. The sun was warm, and I could hear birds singing. He looked at me and smiled and said, "Everything's going to be O.K., you know?" I smiled back, and studied his face as if I was trying desperately to remember a treasure map.

I wanted to remember what he looked like when I awoke, so that in the event I ever saw him again, I could recognize him. His face was handsome, but had ruggedness about him, as did his demeanor at times. He had a sense of being at peace with himself in this place, and he was somehow sharing this with me. I was grateful. I gently placed my hand on top of his against the bed of the truck, and said, "Thank you." He looked at me and smiled and said, "You're going to be alright mate. Everything's going to be alright."

The next morning my youngest little son woke me up. He was standing there with his "holdey blanky" (his security blanket) smiling, and he said in his sweet little voice, "Momma, you're home!" And with that, I was home.

Epilogue

Former Special Agent Catalan and her husband Ben moved their family to a small town back east. There, her and her family live a more tranquil life together as she tries to put this behind her.

Special Agent Ruben Sandoval still works for the Customs agency. Shortly after Darlene left the agency, Ruben was again brought up on more bogus charges and IA investigations, along with the Office Investigative Aid, Yolanda Rios. Ironically, these phony charges were alleged only days after Ruben and Yolanda took part in the reporting of David Gray and Sherry King for the riding while drunk in Gray's G-ride incident. Ruben had taken over the Rail project from Darlene, and he and Renado Gianini tried to cover each other's back, to no avail. The Tanker Car Case, and the Rail Project were again ordered closed by Customs management. When Ruben reported this retaliation to all appropriate agencies, Ruben and Yolanda were subsequently suspended from access to the Department of Treasury's computer systems.

Former Special Agent Sandy Nunn is still leading the fight against Discrimination, Cronyism, and Corruption within the Department of Treasury. Customs blackballed her in the Law Enforcement community, and she had a very hard time getting another job. Sandy, being the resilient fighter that she is, started her own business, and is now doing very well. As hard as all of this has been on her, she is still fighting back with the courage of a tiger in order to keep her promise to her dad. Sandy is in the process of writing a book of her own regarding many of these same issues. Look for "The Dark Side of Justice" due out late summer/fall 2001.

Ricardo Sandoval is still the RAIC (Resident Agent In Charge)/Calexico. Shortly after Customs lost an appeal on Ricardo's lawsuit, the Customs Office of Internal Affairs placed Ricardo under yet another bogus investigation.

Renado Gianini is still a supervisor for the San Bernardino Police Department, Intelligence Unit. He works closely with Ruben, and tries to cover his back.

Ervin Rios is going back to college in evenings and on weekends. He vows to get his law degree, retire from Customs, and protect whistle-blowers against corrupt government managers.

AUSA Yvette Palazuelos has been appointed a Judge in Los Angeles.

Senior Inspector Cathy Harris has been rehired by Customs (only after much pressure/force), and is actively involved with the CEADA (Customs Employees Against Discrimination Association) organization in their fight for justice. Cathy Harris has successfully authored/published a thrilling, accurately portrayed book about her ordeal entitled FLYING WHILE BLACK: A Whistleblower's Story.

Shortly after Darlene resigned, former Inspector and fellow whistle-blower John Carmon of San Diego, California, was arrested on phony charges by the San Diego Police Department. This was also not coincidentally after the meeting with FBI Agent William Motts, and the demonstration at RAIC/Riverside. Although Carmon was arrested by the San Diego Police Department, the arrest was based upon the influence/implication of U.S. Customs Internal Affairs. This was clearly yet another retaliatory act by Customs against Carmon for his whistle blowing activities. All charges have been dismissed against John, and he is pursuing additional legal action against Customs.

SAIC/Los Angeles Drake Brinkley was allowed to retire with full benefits. This was in spite of the fact that numerous violations were reported on him, including evidence/allegations of corruption. Brinkley was recently appointed as a State Gaming Commissioner for a state in the west. Brinkley had also bragged that he is a close friend with Presidential Candidate George W. Bush, and that if Bush is elected Brinkley will be the next Commissioner of Customs.

The Director of Customs Office of Internal Affairs, Harrison Wells, was fired, and a Grand Jury recently indicted him on allegations of perjury and corruption.

Mary Conales is still the Regional EEO Manager for Southern California, in spite of all the numerous well-documented complaints/accusations filed against her.

There has been no disciplinary action (to anyone's knowledge) given to David Gray for the many violations of policy, and attempted rape reported on him.

All allegations in this book have been reported to the F.B.I., The Office of Special Counsel, The Treasury Office of Inspector General, and to numerous members of Congress and the Senate. To date, there has been no Congressional Inquiry into these matters. In December 1999, Former Special Agents Catalan and Sandy Nunn, and Senior Inspector Cathy Harris, along with other Federal Agent whistleblowers, were recently asked to speak at a Town Hall Meeting sponsored by the Rainbow Coalition, in Atlanta, GA. SA Catalan was quoted as saying; "Working for the U.S. Customs Service was like working for the Mafia."

In May 2001, a federal lawsuit was filed on behalf of Sandy Nunn and Darlene Catalan, against the Department of Treasury.

On September 20th, 2001 The Government Accountability Project (GAP) officially read the sworn testimony of Darlene Catalan and Sandy Nunn into the record of a Senate Committee. This was in support of much needed whistleblower legislation.

Notes

GOOD COP BAD COP: By Mike McAlary. This story is about corruption and retaliation against whistleblowers in the NYPD. The Commissioner of the NYPD at the time was Raymond Kelley. Raymond Kelley subsequently became the Commissioner of Customs, and was Commissioner during the timeframe that U.S. CUSTOMS, BADGE OF DISHONOR, and FLYING WHILE BLACK were both written.

FLYING WHILE BLACK: A Whistleblower's Story: By Cathy Harris. Also Cathy Harris has an excellent web sight at: http://cathyharris.homestead.com

Former Customs Inspector, and Customs Whistleblower John Carmon has an excellent web site, a must see for anyone concerned about corruption and the war on drugs: (http://www.customscorruption.com)

Unlimited Access by FBI Agent Gary Aldrich.

Frontline: drug wars: interview John E. Hensley–

Web site (*http://www.pbs.org/wgbh/pages/frontline/shows/drugs/interviews.html*)

Frontline: drug wars: Thirty Years of America's Drug War, a Chronology

web site

(http://www.pbs.org/wgbh/pages/frontline/shows/drugs/cron/index.html)

World Net Daily (*www.WorldNetDaily.com*) articles by Rebecca Hagelin entitled Tracking terrorism dated October 22, 2001 & Train Trouble dated October 16, 2001

NEWS BRIEFS, Law Enforcement section dated January-February 1999, entitled U.S. Customs Service Admits Drug Corruption; Immigration Inspectors Indicted for Drug Corruption (web site–http://www.ndsn.org/JANFEB99/LAWENF.html)

San Antonio Business Journal articles by Bill Conroy entitled U.S. CUSTOMS: Agency whistleblowers getting caught up in Shakespearean tragedy dated May 4, 2001 & Whistlebolwers say nation's railroads should be on red alert, Dated October 8, 2001.

News Max.com–article dated January 20, 2000, entitled: Ex-Customs Agent Exposes Clinton 'Drug War'; Carl Limbacher Jr.; web site (*http://www.newsmax.com/articles/?a=2000/1/20/35428*)

News Max.com–article dated April 20, 1997, entitled: Inspector Alleges Corruption in Customs; Christopher Ruddy web site (http://www.newsmax.com/articles/?a=1997/04/20/151505)

DEA–Publications–Congressional   Testimony–6/24/98;   U.S. Department of Justice, Drug Enforcement Administration–Statement by: Donnie Marshall, DEA

web site (*http://www.usdoj.gov/dea/pubs/cngrtest/ct980624.htm*)

Darlene in Customs office at UPS sight, Ontario Airport

Darlene undercover as DHL delivery person

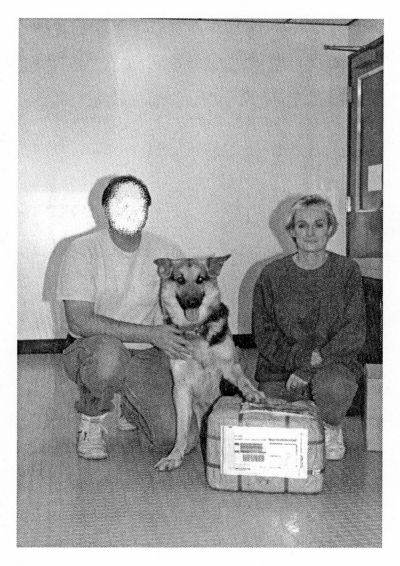

Darlene & seizure of 18lbs of raw opium

Darlene at Long Beach Naval Station

Darlene conducting inspection of suspected alien smugglers.

Printed in the United States
3741